Beginning HCL Programming

Using Hashicorp Language for Automation and Configuration

Pierluigi Riti
David Flynn

Apress®

Beginning HCL Programming: Using Hashicorp Language for Automation and Configuration

Pierluigi Riti
Mullingar, Ireland

David Flynn
New Orleans, LA, USA

ISBN-13 (pbk): 978-1-4842-6633-5
https://doi.org/10.1007/978-1-4842-6634-2

ISBN-13 (electronic): 978-1-4842-6634-2

Managing Director, Apress Media LLC: Welmoed Spahr
Acquisitions Editor: Steve Anglin
Development Editor: Matthew Moodie
Coordinating Editor: Mark Powers

Cover designed by eStudioCalamar

Cover image by Bilge Tekin on Unsplash (www.unsplash.com)

Distributed to the book trade worldwide by Apress Media, LLC, 1 New York Plaza, New York, NY 10004, U.S.A. Phone 1-800-SPRINGER, fax (201) 348-4505, e-mail orders-ny@springer-sbm.com, or visit www. springeronline.com. Apress Media, LLC is a California LLC and the sole member (owner) is Springer Science + Business Media Finance Inc (SSBM Finance Inc). SSBM Finance Inc is a **Delaware** corporation.

For information on translations, please e-mail booktranslations@springernature.com; for reprint, paperback, or audio rights, please e-mail bookpermissions@springernature.com.

Apress titles may be purchased in bulk for academic, corporate, or promotional use. eBook versions and licenses are also available for most titles. For more information, reference our Print and eBook Bulk Sales web page at www.apress.com/bulk-sales.

Any source code or other supplementary material referenced by the author in this book is available to readers on GitHub via the book's product page, located at www.apress.com/9781484266335. For more detailed information, please visit www.apress.com/source-code.

Printed on acid-free paper

Table of Contents

TABLE OF CONTENTS

About the Authors

Pierluigi Riti is a Lead Security Information Engineer and DevOps fanatic he actually work in MasterCard. He has worked for company like, Coupa Software, and Synchronoss Technologies. Prior to that, he was a senior software engineer at Ericsson and Tata. His experience includes implementing DevOps in the cloud using Google Cloud Platform, AWS, and Azure. Also, he has over 20 years of extensive experience in more general design and development of different scale applications particularly in the telco and financial industries. He has quality development skills using the latest technologies including Java, J2EE, C#, F#, .NET, Spring .NET, EF, WPF, WF, WinForm, WebAPI, MVC, Nunit, Scala, Spring, JSP, EJB, Struts, Struts2, SOAP, REST, C, C++, Hibernate, NHibernate, WebLogic, XML, XSLT, Unix script, Ruby, and Python.

David Flynn is an Associate Analyst in Employee Access Business Operations at MasterCard. He is an electronic engineer with experience in telecommunications, networks, software, security, and financial systems. David started out as a telecommunications engineer working on voice, data, and wireless systems for Energis and later Nortel Networks, supporting systems such as Lucent G3r, Alcatel E10, and Nortel Passport. He then did some time in transport and private security abroad before retraining in computing, cyber security, and cloud systems plus doing cyber security and telecomm research for the Civil Service. He has completed separate diplomas in computing and cloud focusing on Windows, C#, Google, AWS, and PowerShell among other technologies. David has also worked as a C# engineer. More recently, David has worked for various fintech companies including Bank of America and Merrill Lynch, focusing on technical and application support encompassing such technologies as Rsa Igl, Rsa SecurID, IBM Tam/Isam, Postgres/Oracle databases, mainframes, Tandem, CyberArk, MaxPro, and Active Directory.

Introduction

HashiCorp offers a full range of products to improve the life of every DevOps engineer. Our goal with this book is to introduce various software applications and show how to use the HCL language to configure them. This book is not meant to be an exhaustive guide to all possible scenarios, but to introduce the software options and how to use them together to create a complete Infrastructure as Code. To get the most out of this book, you should have a basic knowledge of Bash PowerShell scripting and a basic knowledge of programming in general.

CHAPTER 1

Introduction to HCL

HashiCorp is a significant player in the cloud revolution. The company produces most of the essential tools for any DevOps engineer or cloud engineer.

The HashiCorp ecosystem is quite huge; the aim of this book is to introduce the configuration language and the different HashiCorp software components.

HCL, A Brief Introduction

HCL is a configuration language designed to be both human- and machine-readable. HCL is an automation language that is used to manage, create, and release Infrastructure as Code. Based on a study conducted on the GitHub repository, HCL was the third highest in terms of language growth popularity in 2019, which indicates how important the HCL platform has become, which in turn was probably aided by HashiCorp applications like Terraform, Consul, and Vault.

HCL is designed to ease the maintenance of cloud and multi-cloud hybrid solutions. The language is structural, with the goal of being easily understood by humans and machines.

HCL is fully JSON-compatible and the language is intended to be used to build DevOps tools and servers, manage PKI passwords, and release Docker images. HCL gets its inspiration from *libucl*, the Nginx configuration, and other configuration languages.

---

libucl, the Universal Configuration Library Parser, is the main inspiration for the HCL language. As you will see, HCL uses a similar structure, and UCL is heavy inspired by Nginx configuration.

When HCL was designed, the choice was made to mix together the power of a general-purpose language like Ruby, Python, or Java with the simplicity and human readability of JSON. HashiCorp designed its own DSL language.

© Pierluigi Riti and David Flynn 2021
P. Riti and D. Flynn, *Beginning HCL Programming*, https://doi.org/10.1007/978-1-4842-6634-2_1

1

The major usage for HCL is with Terraform. Terraform is HashiCorp's Infrastructure as Code (IaC) or cloud infrastructure automation tool. Both HCL and Terraform enable any DevOps engineer to develop their own tools.

The term *general-purpose language* (GPL) covers the family of programming languages used to develop and design any type of application. This includes Ruby, Python, Go, and Java. On the opposite side are DSLs (domain-specific languages). This family of languages is used in a specific domain, for example, the HTML language. The big difference between a GPL and a DSL language is essentially the use. With a GPL language, we can create and solve any type of problem. A DSL language is designed to solve one specific problem; for example, HTML is used to define how a webpage must be visualized on the screen.

Syntax Overview

HCL comprises a family of DSLs. In this book, we will focus on HCL2, which emphasizes simplicity. HCL has a similar structure to JSON, which allows for a high probability of equivalence between JSON and HCL.

HCL was designed to be JSON-compatible, and every HashiCorp product has a specific call for the relevant API and/or configuration. The entire product suite encompasses this basic syntax. Similar to other languages there are some primitive data types and structures:

- String

- Boolean

- Number

- Tuple

- Object

These are the basic structures and data types that can be used to write HCL code. To create a variable, we can use this syntax: key = value *(the* space doesn't matter). The key is the name of the value, and the value can be any of the primitive types such as string, number, or boolean:

```
description = "This is a String"
number = 1
```

String

The string is defined using the double-quoted syntax and is based (only) on the UTF-8 character set:

```
hello = "Hello World"
```

It is not possible to create a multi-line string. To create multi-line strings, we need to use another syntax.

To create a multi-line string, HCL uses a *here document* syntax, which is a multi-line string starting with << followed by the delimiter identifier (normally a three-letter word like EOF) and succeeded by the same delimiter identifier.

A here document is a file literal or input stream used in particular in the Unix system for adding a multi-line string in a piece of code. Typically this type of syntax starts with << EOF and ends with an EOF.

To create a multi-line string in this way, we can use any text as the delimiter identifier. In this case, it is EOF:

```
<< EOF
Hello
HCL
EOF
```

Number

In HCL, all number data types have a default base of 10, which can be either of the following:

- Integer
- Float

For example,

```
first=10
```

```
second=10.56
```

The variable `first` is an integer number while the variable `second` is a float number. A number can be expressed in hexadecimal by adding the prefix `0x`, octal using the prefix number `0`, or scientific format using `1e10`. For example, we can define the number data types as follows:

```
hexadecimal=0x1E
```

```
octal=07
```

```
scientific=2e15
```

Tuple

HCL supports tuple creation using the square brace syntax, for example:

```
array_test=["first",2,"third"]
```

The value written in an array can be of different types. In the previous example, you can see two string data types and one number data type. In HCL, it is possible to create an array with any type of object:

```
test_array=[true,
    << ERRDOC
      Hello
      Array
    ERRDOC,
    "Test"]
```

Object

In HCL, objects and nested objects can be created using this syntax:

```
<type> <variable/object name> {...}:
.:
```

```
provider "aws" {
      description = "AWS server"
}
```

We can use the same structure for the object to define an *input variable*:

```
variable "provider" {
      name = "AWS"
}
```

Boolean

A Boolean variable in HCL follows the same rules of the other languages. The only value it can have is either true or false:

```
variable "active"{
  value = True
}
```

Comment

A single line of comment can be created using the # or the //:

```
provider "aws" {
      # This is a single line comment
      // This is another single line comment
}
```

To create a multi-line comment, the /*....*/ format can be used:

```
provider "aws" {
      /*
      This is a multi-line comment example
      */
}
```

HIL and HCL

HCL is used for the majority of the use-case scenarios with the Terraform tool. This symbiosis has become a significant factor in the growth of the popularity of HCL.

The HCL that is used to create a template can be translated into JSON by the parser, an important step for creating a valid and usable template for HIL.

HIL, or HashiCorp Interpolating Language, is the language used for *interpolating* any string. It is primarily used in combination with HCL to use a variable defined in other parts of the configuration. HIL uses the syntax ${..} for interpolating the variable, as shown:

```
test = "Hello ${var.world}"
```

The HIL is used to have something similar to a template. This language is mostly used in Terraform. The goal is to have a rich language definition of the infrastructure. The idea behind the creation of HIL was to extract the definition language used in Terraform and then clean it up to create a better and more powerful language.

HIL has its own syntax, which it shares with HCL, such as comments, multi-line comments, Boolean, etc. With HIL, it is possible to create a function for the call, which can be used in the interpolation syntax of the function. This is, in turn, is called with the syntax func(arg1, arg2, ...). For example, we can create a function with the HIL in this way:

```
test = "${ func("Hello", ${hello.var})}"
```

HIL is utilized in more depth when we use Terraform and other software like Nomad.

How HCL Works

You just got a concise introduction to HCL and HIL. But in order to progress beyond this point, you need to create a basic template to illustrate how both components work.

HCL and HIL use the GPL language to create JSON code for the necessary configurations. JSON itself is quite capable of producing the necessary code or configurations so why are HCL/HIL needed? JSON lacks the ability in insert comments, which is essential for reviewing code or configurations, particularly for the massive infrastructure that HCL/HIL is aimed at.

HCL consists of three distinct, integrated sublanguages. All three work together to permit us to create the configuration file:

- *Structural language*

- *Expression language*

- *Template language*

The *structural language* is used to define the overall structure, the hierarchical configuration structure, and its serialization. The three main parts for an HCL snippet are defined as *bodies*, the *block*, and *attributes*.

The *expression language* is used to express the value of the attribute, which can be expressed in either of two ways: a literal or a derivation of another value.

The *template language* is used to compose the value into a string. The template language uses one of the several types of expression defined in the expression language.

When code is composed in HCL, all three sublanguages are normally used. The structural language is used at the top level to define the basis of the configuration file. The expression language and the template language can also be used in isolation or to implement a feature like a REPL, a debugger that can be integrated into more limited HCL syntaxes such as the JSON profile itself.

Syntax Components

A fundamental part of every language is the syntax. Now we'll introduce the basic grammar of HCL and the fundamental parts used to build the language. You've seen which data and type structures are allowed in the HCL language. Now we will delve deeper into syntax. The basic syntax in HCL has these basic rules:

- Every name starting with an uppercase letter is a global production. This means it is common to all syntax specified in the document used to define the program. This is similar to a global variable in other languages.

- Every name starting with a lowercase letter is a local production. This means it is valid only in the part of the document where it is defined. This is similar to a local variable in other languages.

- Double quotes (") or single quotes (') are used to mark a literal character sequence. This can be a punctuation marker or a keyword.

- The default operator for combining items is the *concatenation, the operator +.*

- The symbol | is a logical OR, which means one of the two operators, left or right, must be present.

- The symbol * indicates a "zero or more" repetition of the item on the left. This means we can have a variable number of elements, with the minimum value of 0.

- The symbol ? indicates one or more repetitions of the item to the left.

- The parentheses, ( ) , are used to group items in order to apply the previous operator to them collectively.

These are the basic syntax notations used to define the grammar of the language. They are used in combination with the structure and data types for creating the configuration file(s).

When a HCL configuration file is created, a certain set of rules are used to describe the syntax and grammar involved. There are three distinct sections of the file:

- *Attributes*, where we assign a value to a specific value

- *The block*, which is used to create a child body annotated by a name and an optional label

- *The body content,* which is essentially a collection of attributes and the block

This structure defines the model of the configuration file. A *configuration file* is nothing more than a sequence of characters used to create the body. If we want to define a similar BNF grammar, we can define the basic structure for a configuration file as follows:

```
ConfigFile   = Body;
Body         = (Attribute | Block | OneLineBlock)*;
Attribute    = Identifier "=" Expression Newline;
Block        = Identifier (StringLit|Identifier)* "{" Newline Body "}"
               Newline;
OneLineBlock = Identifier (StringLit|Identifier)* "{" (Identifier "="
               Expression)? "}" Newline;
```

A BNF (Backus-Naur Form) grammar is a notation technique used for free-form grammar. With this technique, we can define a new type of grammar for our own language. This is normally used when we create a new language, like HCL. The BNF is largely used when defining the language and is very helpful when we need to understand the language itself. There is a new version of the BNF called EBFN (Extend-Backus-Naur Form). The BNF is a simple language used in particular in the academic world. There is no unique definition and it is mostly used to describe metacode to be read to a human and is normally written on one line. The EBFN lets us write a more complex model representation of the code; it is possible to define a variable and function with a more complex syntax.

Identifiers

Identifiers are used to assign a name to a block, an attribute, or a variable. An identifier is a string of characters, beginning with a letter or a certain unambiguous punctuation token, followed by any number or letter of Unicode.

The standard used to define an identifier is the Unicode standard, defined in the document UAX #31- Section 2. This document also defines the BNF grammar we can use to write our identifiers. The grammar is as follows:

```
<Identifier> := <Start> <Continue>* (<Medial> <Continue>+)*
```

To define an identifier, this notation is used:

```
Identifier = ID_Start (ID_Continue | '-')*;
```

where

- ID_Start consists of sequence of Unicode letters and certain unambiguous punctuation.

- ID_Continue defines a set of Unicode letters, combining marks and such, as defined in the Unicode standard.

In addition to the first two characters, ID_Start and ID_Continue, we use the character '-'; this character can also be used to define identifiers. The usage of the '-' character allows the identifier to have this character as part of the name.

There is no specific list of reserved words. This is because keywords change depending on the software used to configure.

Operators

In HCL, we have these operators:

```
+   &&   ==   <   :   {   [   (   ${
-   ||   !=   >   ?   }   ]   )   %{
*   !    <=   =   .   /   >=   =>   ,
%   ...
```

All of these operators are used for the logical, mathematical, and structural definitions of the language. As you write configuration files, this will become more apparent.

Numeric Literal

The numeric literal is used to define the structure of a number. The similar BNF notation for a numeric literal is as follows:

```
NumericLit = decimal+ ("." decimal+)? (expmark decimal+)?;
decimal    = '0' .. '9';
expmark    = ('e' | 'E') ("+" | "-")?;
```

Using this syntax, we can define the number like an integer with a non-fractional part plus a fractional part, such as a float number and an exponent part. With the syntax defined previously, we can then write numbers like 0, 0.3, 1e-10, and -10.

Expression

The expression sublanguage is used to create configuration files, specifying values within the attributes definition. The similar BNF specification for the expression is

```
Expression = (
    ExprTerm |
    Operation |
    Conditional
);
```

An expression is normally used to return a type; an expression can return any valid type. The `ExprTerm` is the operator used for the unary and binary expression. `ExprTerm` can act like a normal expression itself. The similar BNF syntax for the `ExprTerm` is

```
ExprTerm = (
    LiteralValue |
    CollectionValue |
    TemplateExpr |
    VariableExpr |
    FunctionCall |
    ForExpr |
    ExprTerm Index |
    ExprTerm GetAttr |
    ExprTerm Splat |
    "(" Expression ")"
);
```

The `ExprTerm` defines a subset of a value and expression. If we use the characters `'` and `'`, we can write a subexpression that follows exactly the same rules as the normal expression. The proceeding sections on values and expressions better illustrate these points. Expressions are used in HCL to define any single piece of the program. There are different types of expressions. One is the conditional expression:

```
condition ? True : False
```

This expression uses a conditional expression to check a value and give a result of True or False. This is essentially an `if...then` or a `for` expression:

```
[for servers in var.list : lower(servers)]
```

The `for...in` is used to check every server in the list, and it's written in all lowercase. There is another type of expression and you'll see it in detail in the rest of the chapter.

LiteralValue

A *literal value* represents the value and the type of a primitive. The literal value defines

- Number
- True or false
- Null

11

The BNF definition for the LiteralValue is similar to

```
LiteralValue = (
  NumericLit |
  "true" |
  "false" |
  "null"
);
```

The literal value does not directly define the string value. It is not directly defined in the LiteralValue. To overcome this, the user is allowed to create a string using the *template language*. The template can then be incorporated to create the string.

CollectionValue

The *collection value* is used to create and define a collection. The BNF syntax to define collection value in comparison is

```
CollectionValue = tuple | object;
tuple = "[" (
    (Expression ("," Expression)* ","?)?
) "]";
object = "{" (
    (objectelem ("," objectelem)* ","?)?
) "}";
objectelem = (Identifier | Expression) "=" Expression;
```

To create a tuple with an object, the tuple is enclosed within [ ], which is similar to an array.

A set of objects can be created using the { and }. When we specify an object, we have the name and the value of the object. For example, we can define an object in this way:

```
{ foo = "Example" }
```

TemplateExpr

A *template expression*, TemplateExpr, embeds a program written in the sublanguage. The program is written as an expression and is normally used in particular in Terraform when we want to define a template.

A template in Terraform is an external file used in Terraform to dynamically load some resource. The template expression can be written in two different forms:

- *Quoted*: This is delimited by the double-quote characters and defines a single-line expression.

- *Heredoc*: This is created using the sequence << or << -. This syntax is used to define the template using a multi-line template.

In the *quoted* template expression, any literal string sequence can be used within the template. It is possible to escape it using the backslash character, \.

The hereDoc template syntax allows for more flexibility during the creation of a template. This is the way to define the template in Terraform; for example, we can use a string form to define a template like this one:

```
data "template_file" "Initialize Consul Address" {
  template = "${file("${path.module}/hcl_book.tpl")}"
  vars = {
    consul_address = "${aws_instance.consul.private_ip}"
  }
}
```

The following code calls a file named hcl_book.tpl. The tpl file is used to define the template expression. The hcl_book.tpl is written like

```
#!/bin/bash

echo "CONSUL_ADDRESS = ${consul_address}" > /tmp/iplist
```

The script reads the CONSUL_ADDRESS configured on the system and writes in the file iplist.

The template file uses the double-quote syntax to define the template expression; the other form used to define the .tpl file is the hereDoc form. The hereDoc form is used to read the data from the template file. We can change the code in this way:

```
user_data = <<-EOT
  echo "CONSUL_ADDRESS = ${aws_instance.consul.private_ip}" > /tmp/iplist
  EOT
```

VariableExpr

The `VariableExpr` is used to define the *variable*. The variable is in the expression and can be defined in its *global scope*. The BNF for a variable is very simple:

```
VariableExpr = Identifier;
```

This syntax is used to create the variable, which in turn allows it to be used in a configuration file.

Function and FunctionCall

A *function* is an operation identified usually with a symbolic name and it solves single or multiple operations as part of an algorithm returning a result.

The namespace of the function is completely different from the namespace of the configuration file. Hence a function and variable can share the same name but this is not advisable because it can cause understandable challenges!

A function is created using the `FunctionCall` syntax. The BNF syntax for the `FunctionCall` is

```
FunctionCall = Identifier "(" arguments ")";
Arguments = (
    () ||
    (Expression ("," Expression)* ("," | "...")?)
);
```

A function is identified by the identifier, the *name* of the function. After the name are the characters (and), and in middle of the parenthesis are the arguments of the function. They are the parameters used in the function to produce the output we want. If the last argument is followed by ..., this means the final argument of the function must be evaluated like a tuple.

HashiCorp define a lot of functions. They can be used to perform basic operations. For example, the function `min()` returns the minimum number:

```
min(12,4,6)
6
```

ForExpr

A `for` expression is a new functionality of HCL2. It is used to read the value from a collection and build another collection.

A `for` expression is used to read a value from a tuple or from an object collection. A `for` expression is used inside a tuple or an object to extract a set of values from the original tuple. For example,

```
[ for value in ["a", "b"]: value]
```

This code returns a new array called `value` with the value ["a","b"]. The position in an array starts at 1.

It is possible to use the `for` expression to read the array and have just the numerical position for the element. To create an array, we can use this syntax for the `for` expression:

```
[for i, value in ["a","b"] : value
```

This syntax returns an array with these values: [1, 2]. It is possible to use an `if` statement to filter on the values selected in the `for` statement:

```
[for i, value in ["a","b","c"] : value if i < 2 ]
```

The code returns ["a","b"].

Index, GetAttr, Splat

The last three components we need to analyze are the index, GetAttr, and splat. An *index* is used to return a value from a tuple, list, or map. It returns a single element from a collection of values. The expression is delimited by the square brackets, [ ], and identified by the expression. It is the *key* we need to get from the list. The key is applied to the list. In a scenario where the key is not present on this list, an error is returned.

The `GetAttr` is an *attribute access operator* which returns a single value from an object. The syntax is an identifier followed by the name of the attributes we want to read from the object.

The last operator is the *splat*. *It's a* unique type of operator which is used to access an element in a list. There are two types of splat operators:

- *Attribute-only*: This splat will look for attributes in a list.
- *Full splat*: This operator supports the indexing into the elements of a list.

The splat operator is used when shorthand for the normal operation is better suited, such as selecting a tuple for an object selection. The splat operator can have a "sugar syntax" for the `for` operator. A normal `for` loop in HCL has this syntax:

```
[for value in tuple: value.foo.bar[1]]
```

Using a splat operator, we can rewrite the `for` to get the same result. The splat operator can be rewritten in this way:

```
tuple[*].foo.bar[1]
```

In the second case, we used the full splat syntax. The operation is equal to `[for value in tuple: value.foo.bar[1]]`.

Conclusion

This chapter provided an introduction to HCL grammar and the BNS used to define the HCL. This is a DSL language that is used in the HashiCorp product suite to create a configuration file. Its notoriety is connected with Terraform. The configuration file is used to create Infrastructure as Code and is fully JSON-compatible. The configuration language can be created by writing a simple file or using some GPL language like Go because HCL uses a parser. To generate the configuration, it is possible use the parser with a GPL language to create the configuration at runtime. In the rest of the book, you will use Go to create a complete configuration file for your Infrastructure as Code. You will see how this can be used to create the configuration file for different HashiCorp products.

CHAPTER 2

The HashiCorp Ecosystem

Since its inception in 2012, HashiCorp's primary mission has been to change how cloud applications are deployed and released.

The company's first application was released in 2010: Vagrant. HashiCorp software is focused on automation and security of infrastructure and hence deployment. Along with Vagrant, other HashiCorp applications were released to enhance this mission. This chapter offers an introduction to these tools.

Defining the Ecosystem

HashiCorp has a very large ecosystem in which every single application is designed to solve a specific challenge. All of the software is open source, including the code itself, which facilitates anyone contributing to actual HashiCorp code fixes. HashiCorp also provides a premium version of its suites for a fee, which is more applicable for enterprises.

All of the tools provided by HashiCorp are intended to support the development and deployment of large-scale service-oriented software systems. Every tool is designed for a specific stage in the software development life cycle. The main products of the suite are as follows:

- *Vagrant* is a tool used to create and maintain a virtual machine environment. Normally this is used for development.

- *Packer* is a tool used to create multiple identical images from a single source. This is used to create customized images for a cloud provider.

- *Terraform*, probably one of the most famous tools, is used to design and develop Infrastructure as Code.

- *Consul* is a tool for network and service discovery.

- *Vault* is a tool for secret management.

© Pierluigi Riti and David Flynn 2021
P. Riti and D. Flynn, *Beginning HCL Programming*, https://doi.org/10.1007/978-1-4842-6634-2_2

- *Nomad* is a tool for scheduling and deploying tasks across a cluster.

- *Serf* is a tool for failure detection, orchestration, and membership management across a cluster.

- *Sentinel* is embedded policy as code for fine-grained logic access.

All of these tools are service oriented and can be used to manage and deploy your Infrastructure as Code. The tools are designed to manage every aspect of software development and deployment and to define the security measures necessary for software release and management. The following sections will cover how to install each of the software tools of the HashiCorp ecosystem.Vagrant

Vagrant was the first tool developed by HashiCorp. Its primary aim is to build a virtual machine environment in a single workflow.

Vagrant provides a convenient way for a developer to create a virtual environment and install it in a different environment. This virtual machine can be installed in different providers like VirtualBox, VMWare, or AWS. When the image is created, you can use any standard tool such as Chef, Puppet, or a simple shell script to release the image into the environment.

Vagrant configures and defines the virtual machine via the `Vagrantfile`. This file defines the resource that can be used and deployed in the virtual machine itself.

Vagrant differs from other virtualization software (like VirtualBox or VMWare) since there is a common CLI tool that can be used to create a virtual machine directly on the command line. With VirtualBox and VMWare, the problem with using the CLI directly is that the software has its own commands and API, so if you want to write general code, you need to write two different programs, one for the API for VirtualBox and one for VMWare.

Vagrant creates a common CLI language, with Vagrant wrapping the specific command for the specific CLI, VirtualBox, and VMWare.

Vagrant allows the developer to create one configuration file called `Vagrantfile`, which can be used with any supported provider, including

- Virtual Box

- VMWare

- Docker

- Hyper-V

This is possible because Vagrant translates the commands into different specific provider calls so the developer can write once and the code is built for everywhere.

Vagrant supports multiple functionalities in order to create and manage the virtual machine. It is possible to create folder synchronization, automatic SSH setup, and an HTTPS tunnel for communicating with the virtual machine. These functions are defined in the Vagrantfile.

Vagrant can be used to create a full development environment. It can be used when a developer needs to create an environment for building and creating the software when Docker is used to create a container entailing a lighter environment but without a lot of the OS functionality enabled. Docker is a perfect choice when you need to create a microservice and you want to enable a full CI/CD circle.

Downloading and Installing Vagrant

The best way to understand software is to get your hands dirty. For this reason, the next step is to download and install Vagrant on your computer.

Vagrant needs a *provider* to work properly. A provider is software that is used to create a virtual machine like VirtualBox or VMWare. Vagrant uses the provider to create the image and then start the image. Because VirtualBox is free software, we suggest installing it; go to www.virtualbox.org/wiki/Downloads. After you install VirtualBox, you can download and install Vagrant. Be sure to have the provider software installed first.

To download Vagrant, follow this link: www.vagrantup.com/downloads.html.

Select the version of Vagrant to download, as shown Figure 2-1, depending on your operating system. Follow the instructions and install it.

We used Windows machines, so the screenshots in this book are based on Windows installations, but the steps are the same for any operating system.

Figure 2-1. *The Vagrant download page for selecting the operating system*

Start the Vagrant installation file; input your drive and desired location, as shown in Figure 2-2.

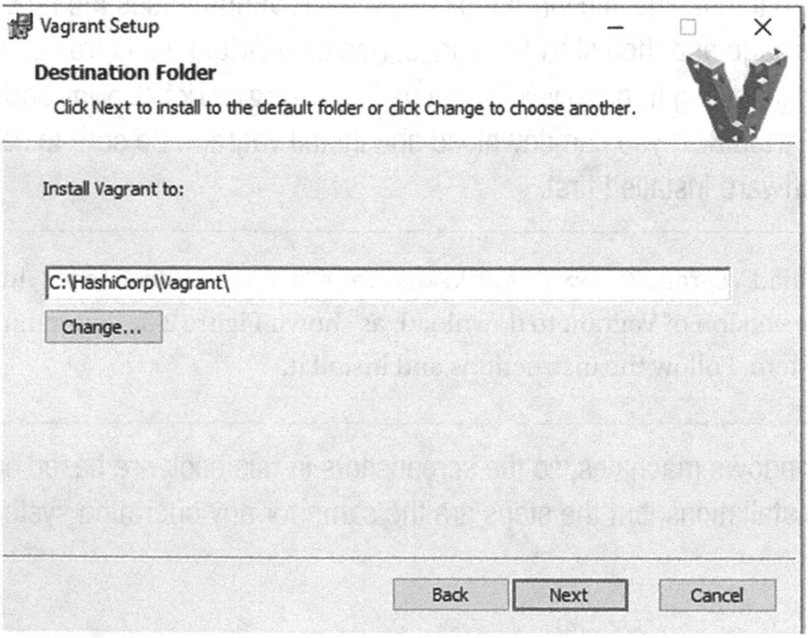

Figure 2-2. *Selecting the path during the Vagrant installation*

Press the Next button. Start the Vagrant installation by pressing Install. The installation will start. See Figure 2-3.

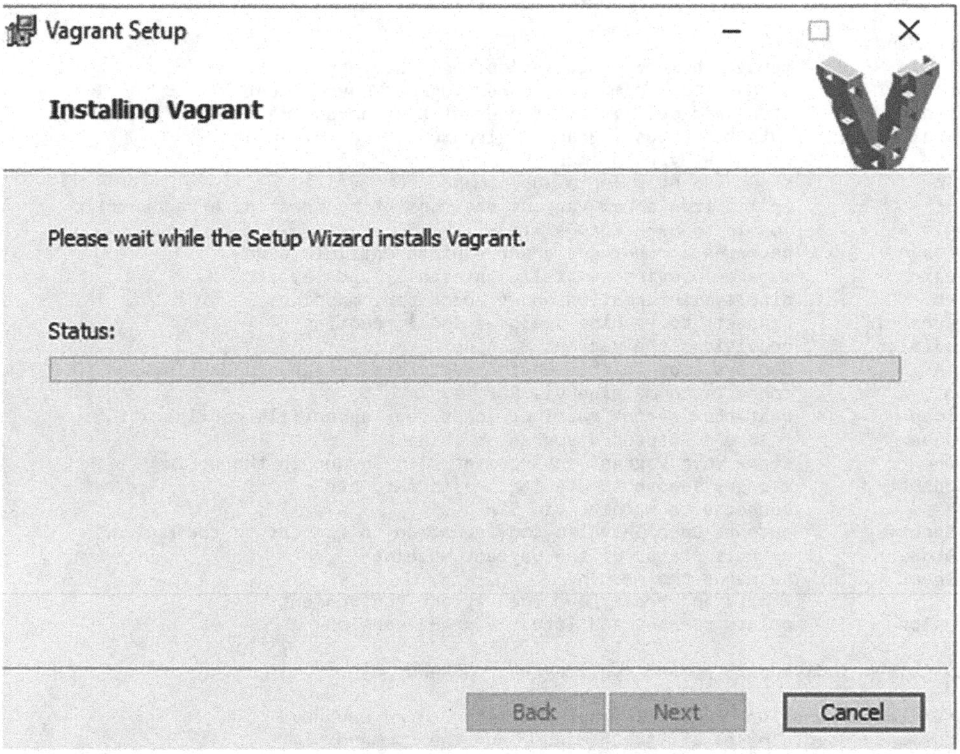

Figure 2-3. *The Vagrant installation status*

When the installation is finished, restart your computer. Successful installation can be verified by running the vagrant -h command on the command line. The output should return the Vagrant help options shown in Figure 2-4.

```
C:\Users\Pierluigi>vagrant -h
Usage: vagrant [options] <command> [<args>]

   -v, --version                    Print the version and exit.
   -h, --help                       Print this help.

Common commands:
      box            manages boxes: installation, removal, etc.
      connect        connect to a remotely shared Vagrant environment
      destroy        stops and deletes all traces of the vagrant machine
      global-status  outputs status Vagrant environments for this user
      halt           stops the vagrant machine
      help           shows the help for a subcommand
      init           initializes a new Vagrant environment by creating a Vagrantfile
      login          log in to HashiCorp's Atlas
      package        packages a running vagrant environment into a box
      plugin         manages plugins: install, uninstall, update, etc.
      port           displays information about guest port mappings
      powershell     connects to machine via powershell remoting
      provision      provisions the vagrant machine
      push           deploys code in this environment to a configured destination [DEPRECATED]
      rdp            connects to machine via RDP
      reload         restarts vagrant machine, loads new Vagrantfile configuration
      resume         resume a suspended vagrant machine
      share          share your Vagrant environment with anyone in the world
      snapshot       manages snapshots: saving, restoring, etc.
      ssh            connects to machine via SSH
      ssh-config     outputs OpenSSH valid configuration to connect to the machine
      status         outputs status of the vagrant machine
      suspend        suspends the machine
      up             starts and provisions the vagrant environment
      version        prints current and latest Vagrant version

For help on any individual command run `vagrant COMMAND -h`

Additional subcommands are available, but are either more advanced
or not commonly used. To see all subcommands, run the command
`vagrant list-commands`.
```

Figure 2-4. *The Vagrant help options*

With Vagrant up and running, let's take a look at the basic usage.

Vagrant First Usage

Vagrant is very user friendly when the objective is to create a development environment with the added facility of testing. Open the Vagrant command line interface. As shown in Figure 2-5, select the folder to maintain your Box. In this example, create a folder named IntroductionHCL. Then enter this command:

```
vagrant init hashicorp/bionic64
```

This command will download and configure the `hashicorp/bionic64` Vagrant Box. This will create a full Ubuntu 18.04 LTS 64-bit with a `Vagrantfile` in the folder. (`Vagrantfile` is the configuration file used by Vagrant to create and define the resource for your Box). See Listing 2-1.

Listing 2-1. The Vagrant init Command Result

```
A `Vagrantfile` has been placed in this directory. You are now
ready to `vagrant up` your first virtual environment! Please read
the comments in the Vagrantfile as well as documentation on
`vagrantup.com` for more information on using Vagrant.
```

To spin up the virtual machine using this downloaded image, run the command `vagrant up`.

Sometimes Vagrant doesn't recognize the VirtualBox installation and will show an error about the provider not being found. In this case, the solution is to uninstall and reinstall VirtualBox and use the `vagrant up` command again.

The command `vagrant up` creates a new virtual machine in your provider. The next step is to download the image for the specific provider, in your case VirtualBox. With the downloaded image, create a new virtual machine.

```
Bringing machine 'default' up with 'virtualbox' provider...
==> default: Box 'hashicorp/bionic64' could not be found. Attempting to
    find and install...
    default: Box Provider: virtualbox
    default: Box Version: >= 0
==> default: Loading metadata for box 'hashicorp/precise64'
    default: URL: https://vagrantcloud.com/hashicorp/precise64
==> default: Adding box 'hashicorp/bionic64' (v1.1.0) for provider:
            virtualbox
    default: Downloading: https://vagrantcloud.com/hashicorp/boxes/
            bionic64/versions/1.1.0/providers/virtualbox.box
    default: Download redirected to host: vagrantcloud-files-production.
            s3.amazonaws.com
    default:
```

```
==> default: Successfully added box 'hashicorp/bionic64' (v1.1.0) for
              'virtualbox'!
==> default: Importing base box 'hashicorp/bionic64'...
==> default: Matching MAC address for NAT networking...
==> default: Checking if box 'hashicorp/bionic64' version '1.1.0' is up to
              date...
==> default: Setting the name of the VM: IntroductionHCL_
              default_1567362265579_87790
==> default: Fixed port collision for 22 => 2222. Now on port 2200.
==> default: Clearing any previously set network interfaces...
==> default: Preparing network interfaces based on configuration...
    default: Adapter 1: nat
==> default: Forwarding ports...
    default: 22 (guest) => 2200 (host) (adapter 1)
==> default: Running 'pre-boot' VM customizations...
==> default: Booting VM...
==> default: Waiting for machine to boot. This may take a few minutes...
    default: SSH address: 127.0.0.1:2200
    default: SSH username: vagrant
    default: SSH auth method: private key
    default:
    default: Vagrant insecure key detected. Vagrant will automatically
              replace
    default: this with a newly generated keypair for better security.
    default:
    default: Inserting generated public key within guest...
    default: Removing insecure key from the guest if it's present...
    default: Key inserted! Disconnecting and reconnecting using new SSH
              key...
==> default: Machine booted and ready!
==> default: Checking for guest additions in VM...
    default: The guest additions on this VM do not match the installed
              version of
    default: VirtualBox! In most cases this is fine, but in rare cases it can
```

```
    default: prevent things such as shared folders from working properly.
        If you see
    default: shared folder errors, please make sure the guest additions
        within the
    default: virtual machine match the version of VirtualBox you have
        installed on
    default: your host and reload your VM.
    default:
    default: Guest Additions Version: 4.2.0
    default: VirtualBox Version: 6.0
==> default: Mounting shared folders...
    default: /vagrant => C:/IntroductionHCL
```

If you open VirtualBox, you will see the new virtual machine created (see Figure 2-5).

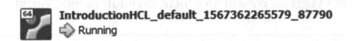

Figure 2-5. *The virtual image created in VirtualBox*

The virtual machine is now created. To access it, use the command

```
vagrant ssh
```

This command opens an SSH session on the existing virtual machine and allows you to use the image as a new operating system. You can see the result of the command ssh below:

```
C:\IntroductionHCL>vagrant ssh
Welcome to Ubuntu 18.04 LTS (GNU/Linux 3.2.0-23-generic x86_64)

Welcome to your Vagrant-built virtual machine.
Last login: Fri Sep 14 06:23:18 2012 from 10.0.2.2
vagrant@bionic64:~$
```

Now you'll see a new Ubuntu environment inside your operating system. When you exit from the Unix OS, the box doesn't stop; it's still running in the background. The following command will show all boxes installed on Vagrant:

```
vagrant box list
```

If you run the command, you'll only see the box you created previously:

```
C:\IntroductionHCL>vagrant box list
hashicorp/bionic64 (virtualbox, 1.1.0)
```

It is possible shut down the virtual machine with the command

```
vagrant halt
```

This command will shut down the virtual machine that is actually running. The result is shown below:

```
C:\IntroductionHCL>vagrant halt
==> default: Attempting graceful shutdown of VM...
```

We have now finished our short introduction to Vagrant. This book is not intended to teach you everything about Vagrant. We will now focus on another tool: Terraform.

Terraform

Terraform is probably the most well-known and most often used tool developed by HashiCorp. This tool has grown in popularity with the cloud.

Terraform is used to install, manage, configure, and create different versions of the infrastructure in a consistent manner. This means that with Terraform, if you don't change anything in the definition file, the result is always the same.

When you change the definition in the Terraform file, you still version your infrastructure. This means you can have different file for creating different infrastructures, such as different version of the operating system or the software installed in the infrastructure itself. Terraform can manage existing infrastructure in the cloud using the most popular providers, such as AWS, Google, Azure, or your in-house infrastructure, like for an OpenStack or VMWare virtual infrastructure.

Key Features of Terraform

Terraform is able to configure a single server or an entire datacenter. Listing 2-2 shows a configuration file for Terraform.

Listing 2-2. A Terraform Configuration File Example

```
provider "aws" {
  profile = "default"
  region  = "us-east-1"
}

resource "aws_instance" "terraform_example" {
  ami           = "downloading-2757f631"
  instance_type = "t2.micro"
}
```

The configuration file shows how to create a new AWS instance in us-east-1 and assign the instance an ami and instance type, which is used to create the instance directly in AWS. Terraform can directly translate the configuration file into the correct API call for creating the instance in AWS. Terraform has some unique key features:

- *Infrastructure as Code:* The infrastructure is defined using a high-level configuration, which allows the release and versioning of infrastructure like another piece of software. In addition, because the infrastructure is defined in a repo, you can easily reuse this code, hence infrastructure.

- *An execution plan*: Terraform can define "planning" steps, which are common in some software for software building and release, like Capistrano. The result is an execution plan where Terraform shows all the steps needed to execute the creation and release the infrastructure as code.

- *Resource graph:* Terraform creates a graph with all the resources. The installation follows a parallelized creation and modification of any non-dependent resource that accelerates the creation of your infrastructure plus the operators get a deep look into the infrastructure dependencies.

- *Change automation:* With Terraform, you can easily apply very complex change sets. The resource graph allows the easy tracking of dependencies across the infrastructure. This helps to reduce human error by showing exactly each stage.

This process will become clearer in the following sections as you install and experiment with the application.

Installing Terraform

The first step is to download the Terraform binaries file from `www.terraform.io/downloads.html`. Select the appropriate file depending on your operating system and then download the file. See Figure 2-6.

Figure 2-6. *The Terraform installation platform*

After downloading the file, unzip the file in a folder and configure the path. For example, create the folder `TerraformHCL` under the root of the computer and unzip the file in the folder, as in Figure 2-7.

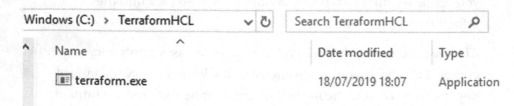

Figure 2-7. *The folder where Terraform is actually installed*

The next step is to make Terraform available on your environment. Configure the path to the folder. So in Windows, this would be as shown in Figure 2-8.

Figure 2-8. *The configuration you need to add in the path*

Finally, you can test your Terraform configuration by opening a command line and running the command `terraform`. The result should show the help menu/list:

```
C:\Users\Pierluigi>terraform
Usage: terraform [-version] [-help] <command> [args]
```

The available commands for execution are listed below. The most common, useful commands are shown first, followed by the less common or more advanced commands. If you're just getting started with Terraform, stick with the common commands. For the other commands, please read the help and docs before usage.

```
Common commands:
    apply              Builds or changes infrastructure, this essentially
    create             the infrastructure defined in the plan
    console            Interactive console for Terraform interpolations
    destroy            Destroy Terraform-managed infrastructure
    env                Workspace management
    fmt                Rewrites config files to canonical format, this command
                       apply some transformation for have a correct style
    get                Download and install modules for the configuration
    graph              Create a visual graph of Terraform resources
    import             Import existing infrastructure into Terraform
    init               Initialize a Terraform working directory, this
                       command need to be run first of any other command,
                       and this commands do some basic configuration steps
                       in the folder.
    output             Read an output from a state file
    plan               Generate and show an execution plan
    providers          Prints a tree of the providers used in the configuration
    refresh            Update local state file against real resources
```

show	Inspect Terraform state or plan
taint	Manually mark a resource for recreation
untaint	Manually unmark a resource as tainted
validate	Validates the Terraform files
version	Prints the Terraform version
workspace	Workspace management

All other commands:

0.12upgrade	Rewrites pre-0.12 module source code for v0.12
debug	Debug output management (experimental)
force-unlock	Manually unlock the terraform state
push	Obsolete command for Terraform Enterprise legacy (v1)
state	Advanced state management

You can check the version of Terraform using the command

```
terraform version
```

The result is the version of Terraform you actually installed, which in our case is 0.12.7:

```
C:\Users\Pierluigi>terraform version
Terraform v0.12.7
```

You have now Terraform installed on your environment. We will revisit Terraform at a later stage in the book. Let's move onto another HashiCorp product: Vault.

Vault

Vault is dedicated to solving some of the security issues associated with the adoption of the cloud. In a dedicated data center, we know who secures the systems. However, in the cloud, we don't know how many people have access to our data and what level of security skills the personnel have. In addition, because others work in the company and thus could access the data, we don't really have a list of people who can access the data, and this can expose us to hacking because an internal employee of the cloud company could do damage or steal our data. Vault encrypts the data you store in it and make this data inaccessible to other people and other secret engines.

Key Features of Vault

It is possible to create and manage the security secrets of your Infrastructure as Code in the cloud using Vault:

- *Secrets management*: Vault is designed to maintain and manage secrets such API keys, SSH keys, passwords, certificates, and much more. With Vault, it is easy to store and manage the secrets for use across the cloud.

- *Identity and access management:* Vault uses a different way to ensure correct access of the system. With Vault, you can define different types of policies. For example, you can have the same level of access to the secrets as you have in other environments.

- *Encryption as a Service:* Data can be protected in transit or at rest. An important feature for any company concerned about security, this feature is used when you create a transit secret engine. The data is not stored in Vault, but is encrypted when in "transit" from one user to another. So if there is a data breach, the data is completely encrypted.

These Vault features can easily be integrated with a cloud provider, and at the same time Vault can be integrated with your normal development to enhance the security of the system.

Like any other HashiCorp software, Vault can be configured using a HCL file; see Listing 2-3.

Listing 2-3. A Vault HCL Configuration File

```
storage "consul" {
  address = "127.0.0.1:8500"
  path    = "vault"
}

listener "tcp" {
  address     = "127.0.0.1:8200"
  tls_disable = 1
}
```

```
telemetry {
  statsite_address = "127.0.0.1:8125"
  disable_hostname = true
}
```

The configuration file follows the same structure of all the other applications shown up to now. The next step is to install Vault on your machine.

Installing Vault

Vault can be installed by downloading the latest binaries for your operating system from `www.vaultproject.io/downloads.html`. Select the operating system and then download the binary for that operating system. See Figure 2-9.

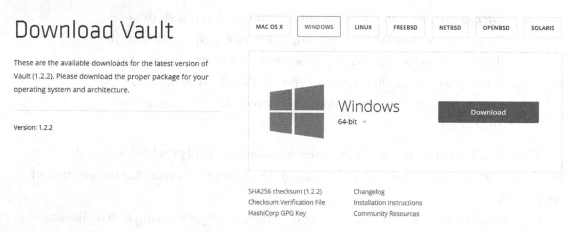

Figure 2-9. *The Vault download page*

Decompress the downloaded file to the root folder. Vault runs as a single binary. Configure the path as shown in Figure 2-10.

Figure 2-10. *The Vault value configured on the path*

To confirm the installation, open the command line and use the command shown in Listing 2-4.

Listing 2-4. The Vault Command

```
'vault'. The result is the manual for the Vault software:
Usage: vault <command> [args]

Common commands:
    read       Read data and retrieves secrets
    write      Write data, configuration, and secrets
    delete     Delete secrets and configuration
    list       List data or secrets
    login      Authenticate locally
    agent      Start a Vault agent
    server     Start a Vault server
    status     Print seal and HA status
    unwrap     Unwrap a wrapped secret

Other commands:
    audit        Interact with audit devices
    auth         Interact with auth methods
    kv           Interact with Vault's Key-Value storage
    lease        Interact with leases
    namespace    Interact with namespaces
    operator     Perform operator-specific tasks
    path-help    Retrieve API help for paths
    plugin       Interact with Vault plugins and catalog
    policy       Interact with policies
    print        Prints runtime configurations
    secrets      Interact with secrets engines
    ssh          Initiate an SSH session
    token        Interact with tokens
```

Once you have validated the Vault installation, its utilization can be shown. In the context of Infrastructure as Code, Vault can manage the secrets and the other security configurations used in the coding. For example, it can be used with a transit secret engine to have encryption only on the data in transit.

Consul

Consul is a tool used for the service mesh and is offered via a full control plane for service discovery, service configuration, and segmentation.

A service mesh is a software architecture used to create a dedicated layer for facilitating service communication, such as a microservice. The service mesh layer is used to facilitate communication between the services.

With Consul, it is possible to create a service mesh layer and use some of the Consul features individually or in a combination with other features.

Using the features in combination allows the creation of a full-service mesh functionality.

Consul is shipped with a built-in proxy but it also supports a third-party proxy such as Envoy. Consul has some key features:

- *Service discovery:* A client can use Consul to register a service such as an API or MySQL. Another client can use Consul to discover the service they need.

- *Health service checking:* Consul can monitor the status of a service and raise an error when the service goes down.

- *Key/value store:* Consul can be used to store key/value pairs. This can be used to store a feature associated with a key (like a DNS).

- *Secure service communication*: Consul can distribute TLS certificates for a service to allow secure communication.

Consul is used as a distributed system where each node has a *Consul agent*. The agent is not required for service discovery or other features. Its only responsibility is to perform a health check on all services on the *Consul server*. The Consul server holds the data, which is replicated across different nodes.

Nomad

Another important tool developed by HashiCorp is Nomad, which is a workload orchestrator. By using Nomad you can easily deploy any container or legacy application.

You can create a declarative Infrastructure as Code that can be used to define and orchestrate a Docker microservice plus other legacy software in your infrastructure. The key features of the tool are the following:

- *Deploying containers and legacy applications:* Easily deploy different type of applications in the same simple configuration file.

- *Device and plugin support:* Nomad can be used for machine learning and AI. It offers native support for the GPU.

- *Multi-region federation support:* Nomad natively supports multi-region federation, allowing for deployment of multiple data centers across different regions.

Nomad is fully integrated into the HashiCorp ecosystem, which allows easy integration with Terraform, Vault, and Consul to implement full Infrastructure as Code to a high-security standard.

Conclusion

This was a short introduction to the HashiCorp ecosystem. We showed the complete set of tools needed for cloud and enterprise applications.

All of these tools have in common the HashiCorp configuration language, which can be programmed via the API to parse the language and install the software.

Each tool can be used individually or in conjunction with others for a complete solution. In the following chapters, we will introduce Go and explain how to use it to manipulate and programmatically create a configuration file for use in the HashiCorp ecosystem.

CHAPTER 3

Introduction to Go

Go is a general-purpose open-source language. Officially launched at the end of 2009, Go was initially an internal Google Project which took its inspiration from other languages like C, Pascal, and Alef. The central objective of Go was to create a language for the professional user who wants to create robust software seamlessly.

Go has steadily grown in popularity, becoming the fifth most used language for the IEEE and seventh for GitHub. Go has very rich libraries which allow you to easily build complex software on the Web with Unix/system management.

First Steps with Go

The best way to learn Go is to try it. It is possible use Go without installing it. In this section, you will see some basic Go commands and program structure. To start Go, go to `https://tour.golang.org/welcome/1`. On the right of the page is a small window where it is possible to write a small Go program and test it; see Figure 3-1.

© Pierluigi Riti and David Flynn 2021
P. Riti and D. Flynn, *Beginning HCL Programming*, https://doi.org/10.1007/978-1-4842-6634-2_3

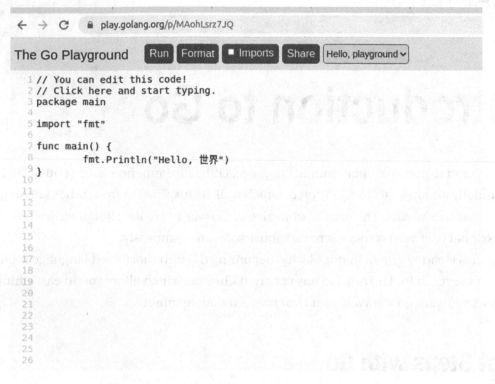

Figure 3-1. *The Go Site for Testing the Language*

In the session "Try Go," you can read a basic Go program. See Listing 3-1.

Listing 3-1. A Basic Go Program

```
// You can edit this code!
// Click here and start typing. (1)
package main (2)

import "fmt" (3)

func main() { (4)
  fmt.Println("Hello, 世界") (5)
}
```

This basic program describes the basic structure for a Go program. Line (1) shows how to insert a single-line comment in Go. Similar to other languages, you use the // characters followed by the comment.

Every program in Go needs to have a package. The basic package is the main section; in line (2) you see how to start every Go program. The `package main` is where the main method resides and every Go program starts here. Line (3) shows the import, which is used to import other packages into program. The `fmt` package is the basic I/O functionality for the program. In this case, it is used to write the output on line (5). From the package `fmt` you use the `Println` function, which is used to write out a message and add a newline.

In line (4) you define a basic function in Go: the function has this syntax: `func <name>() {`. After the definition every function in Go needs a closing `}`. This is one of differences from other languages. In Go, the `{` sign must be on the same line of the function definition. To run, press the Run button. The result of the program is shown in the window below the code; see Figure 3-2.

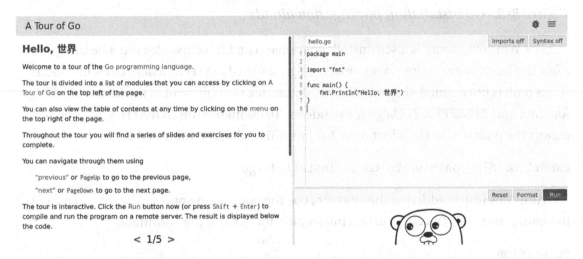

Figure 3-2. *The result of the basic program*

You can continue to explore Go using the playground offered on the site, but to progress in this book, you need to install it in your environment, so let's do it!

Installing Go

Go can be installed on all major operating systems. Download the applicable package by pressing the Download Go button. The website `https://golang.org/dl/` provides installers for each OS. See Figure 3-3.

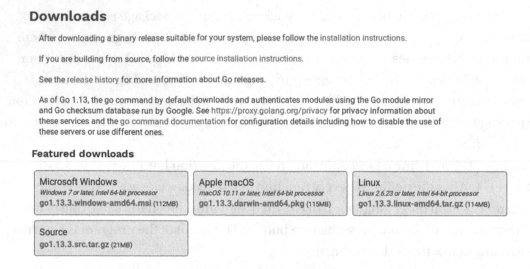

Downloads

After downloading a binary release suitable for your system, please follow the installation instructions.

If you are building from source, follow the source installation instructions.

See the release history for more information about Go releases.

As of Go 1.13, the go command by default downloads and authenticates modules using the Go module mirror and Go checksum database run by Google. See https://proxy.golang.org/privacy for privacy information about these services and the go command documentation for configuration details including how to disable the use of these servers or use different ones.

Featured downloads

Microsoft Windows	Apple macOS	Linux
Windows 7 or later, Intel 64-bit processor	macOS 10.11 or later, Intel 64-bit processor	Linux 2.6.23 or later, Intel 64-bit processor
go1.13.3.windows-amd64.msi (112MB)	go1.13.3.darwin-amd64.pkg (115MB)	go1.13.3.linux-amd64.tar.gz (114MB)

Source		
go1.13.3.src.tar.gz (21MB)		

Figure 3-3. *Go installation package downloads*

For Windows, there is a self-installer package. The Linux installer must be unzipped. After the installation is done, you must configure the GOPATH to where Go is installed. If this path is not defined, the compiler will determine Go is present in the folder %HOME%/go for Unix and %USERPROFILE%/go for Windows. To configure the GOPATH, you need to export the path where Go is installed. In Unix, this is done in the .bashrc file:

```
export GOPATH=<path where Go is installed>/go
```

After this line is added to the .bashrc, use the command source .bashrc to reload the command line. To verify correct installation for Go, use the command

```
go version
```

This command will show the actual version of Go applicable to that operating system:

```
go version go1.13.1 linux/amd64
```

For your first program, open a text editor and write the program shown in Listing 3-2.

Listing 3-2. A "Hello World" Program

```
package main

import "fmt"

func main() {
  fmt.Println("Hello, World")
}
```

Save the file with the name `HelloWorld.go`. To run the file, use the command `go run <name of the Go file>`. In your case, the command is

```
go run HelloWorld.go
```

The result of the command is the execution of the main, shown in Listing 3-3.

Listing 3-3. The Command Line Executed for the Go Run

```
piggi@piggi:~/Desktop$ go run HelloWorld.go

Hello, World
```

You just created a basic program in Go in your test environment. It is now time to learn the basic syntax of the language.

Starting with Go

Learning Go offers the following advantages:

- Go has garbage collection, which means the developer doesn't need to manage memory.

- Go doesn't have a preprocessor. Compilation is therefore faster and expands the use case of Go as a scripting language.

- Go by default uses static linking. This means when the program is compiled for a specific OS, the complied file can be moved and executed in another OS, of course of the same family, without modification.

41

These are just some of the advantages of using Go to write programs. With Go is possible to write simple program for Network development, to write more complex program like piece of code for Operating System development.

Go has two simple rules, which are designed to reduce the bugs in the code:

- Import only the packages you are going to use.

- The bracket must stay after the name of the function.

These rules help maintain clear and understandable code across the different teams in a project.

Go Packages

Like every language, Go uses packages to organize the code to allow the developer to import libraries. The first rule of the language is to import a package only when you use it. If you import a package and you don't use it in the code, the compiler will raise an exception.

```
import(
        "package1"
        "package2"
        ....
        )
```

This syntax allows the importation of more than one package at the same time. When you compile and run it, an error is raised:

```
package main

import (
        "fmt"
        "os"
)

func main() {
        fmt.Println("Hello World!")
}
```

If you run this program, the console will return with an error of "Unused import OS."

To run and compile a Go program, use the command `build`. It essentially compiles the package and all of the dependencies. You can run the program using the code in Listing 3-4.

Listing 3-4. The Go Error for an Unused Import

```
go build import_rule.go
piggi@piggi:~/Desktop/HCL_Book/code/chapter_3$ go build import_rule.go
# command-line-arguments
./import_rule.go:5:2: imported and not used: "os"
```

Sometimes you may need to import packages for use later. With Go, it is possible to declare a package using the prefix _ before the package name. This will negate the compiler error:

```
package main

import (
        "fmt"
        _"os"
)

func main() {
        fmt.Println("Hello World!")
}
```

This time the compiler won't raise an error, as shown in Listing 3-5.

Listing 3-5. The Code with the Syntax for Ignoring the Package

```
piggi@piggi:~/Desktop/HCL_Book/code/chapter_3$ go build import_rule.go
piggi@piggi:~/Desktop/HCL_Book/code/chapter_3$
```

If you want to use the library, you need to remove the underscore (_) in front of the imported library; otherwise, Go will raise an error about a missing import.

Although Go has access to extensive libraries, access to an external library is sometimes needed. In Go, you can directly reference the GitHub link where the library is hosted:

```
import(
      "fmt"
      "github.com/gorilla/mux"
      )
```

The code shows how to import an external library in Go but first you need to be sure to have the library in your GOPATH or GOROOT or downloaded locally already. To download the package locally, use this simple Go command:

```
go get -v <github package>
```

For the previous package, this is the command to import the package in your own system:

```
go get -v  github.com/gorilla/mux
```

If you don't download the package, the compiler will raise an exception for the missing package, as shown in Listing 3-6.

Listing 3-6. Example of External Import in Go

```
package main

import (
      "net/http"

      "github.com/gorilla/mux"
)

func main() {
      r := mux.NewRouter()
      http.Handle("/", r)
}
```

When you run the code, the compiler will raise the exception shown in Listing 3-7.

Listing 3-7. The Error Raised by Go for the Missing Package

```
piggi@piggi:~/Desktop/HCL_Book/code/chapter_3$ go build external_import.go
external_import.go:6:2: cannot find package "github.com/gorilla/mux" in any of:
        /usr/local/go/src/github.com/gorilla/mux (from $GOROOT)
        /home/piggi/Projects/src/github.com/gorilla/mux (from $GOPATH)
```

To fix the issue, you must import the package into your environment, as shown in Listing 3-8.

Listing 3-8. The Import for the Missing Library

```
piggi@piggi:~/Desktop/HCL_Book/code/chapter_3$ go get -v  github.com/
gorilla/mux
github.com/gorilla/mux (download)
github.com/gorilla/mux
```

With the library now imported, you can run the program without any error:

```
piggi@piggi:~/Desktop/HCL_Book/code/chapter_3$ go build external_import.go
piggi@piggi:~/Desktop/HCL_Book/code/chapter_3$
```

To delete the package from the system when it is no longer necessary, do this:

```
go clean -i -v -x  github.com/gorilla/mux
```

When you run this command, Go deletes the package from the system. You can reimport it if you need it. The result of the command is shown in Listing 3-9.

Listing 3-9. The Command for Removing a Package in Go

```
piggi@piggi:~/Desktop/HCL_Book/code/chapter_3$ go clean -i -v -x
github.com/gorilla/mux
cd /home/piggi/Projects/src/github.com/gorilla/mux
rm -f mux.test mux.test.exe
rm -f /home/piggi/Projects/pkg/linux_amd64/github.com/gorilla/mux.a
```

Basic Programming Structure

Like every other programming language, a Go program is built using a series of small instructions. You saw an example of this in the previous section when you wrote your first Go program. The rest of the chapter will detail how a Go program is built.

Naming Conventions

A program is made up of a set of variables, functions, and data within an algorithm to achieve a specific objective. Every variable and function must have a name, which in Go is defined as follows:

- A name must begin with a letter or an underscore.

- The name continues with an arbitrary number of letters, numbers, or underscores.

- Go is case sensitive, so *testName* and *testname* are two different names.

Go has some conventions for writing programs. Go uses a camelCase style (this means the variable uses a mix of lowercase and uppercase letters for defining the name of the entity), such as *firstFunction*. This style prefers an interior uppercase letter instead of an underscore.

Variables

The building block of every program is a variable. This is probably the entity most used in any program. The basic syntax for defining a variable is

var <name> <type> = <value>

The word `var` is used to define the variable in the language. After the `var` keyword, you define the name of the variable and then the type. Optionally, you can assign a value on the variable when it is defined:

```
var s string
var maximum string
var number int
```

Go has the ability to type interference the variable, which means you can declare the variable without specifying the type and, during the assignation of the value, the compiler is able to determine the type of the variable. With Go, it is also possible to initialize a set of variables.

```
var s = "hello" //string
var k,s,m = 10, "hello", 10.0 //int, string, float64
```

Go has another way of defining a variable. This is called the *short variable declaration* and is done using the operator := like so:

```
number := 100
freq := rand.Float64() * 5
```

This type of declaration is used in particular when you need to define a local variable. The var word is used in particular to definite a variable at a global level or when the variable is not directly initialized.

Pointers

Pointers are strictly connected to the variable. When a *variable is defined*, the compiler uses a piece of memory to store the value. The pointer is the address of the memory used to store the value or the pointer value is the address of the variable. With a pointer, it is possible to change the value of a variable without performing a direct assign to the variable since the pointer works directly on the memory assigned to the variable.

The syntax for creating and using the pointer is quite different from that of a variable. To clarify how a pointer works, let's analyze the simple piece of code in Listing 3-10.

Listing 3-10. Using a Pointer

```
package main

import (
        "fmt"
)
```

```go
func main() {
    x := 1                 // Declare the variable x and assign the value 1
    p := &x                // create a pointer to x the type is *int
    fmt.Println(*p)        // Write the value of the pointer p
    *p = 2                 // the new value of x is 2, this because *p
                           //    "point" the address memory of x

    fmt.Println(x)
}
```

The program shows how to use a pointer. If you execute the program, you will get this result:

```
piggi@piggi:~/Desktop/HCL_Book/code/chapter_3$ go run pointer.go
1
2
```

The pointer is created with the syntax &x, which means "address of x." The expression &x gets the address of the x and assigns it to the variable pointer p. It is possible to read the "value" of the memory with the syntax *p. This syntax reads the value of the address of memory. Similarly to reading the value, you can also assign a new value to the memory; this is done simply by assigning to the pointer *p a new value, in this case, 2.

Pointers are widely used in Go. They are very powerful and facilitate creating a program in a minimal amount of time. There will be further examples of how pointers help in the creation of better and efficient code.

Go Data Types

Every language has some basic data types. They are used to compose complicated data structures. In Go, there are essentially four categories of data types:

- *Basic types*: These types include strings, numbers, and Booleans.

- *Composite types*: This type of data can be split into two subcategories.

    - *Non-reference types*: These types include arrays and structs.

    - *Reference types*: These types include pointers, maps, slices, functions, and channels.

- *Interface type*: This is a normal interface.

In the rest of the chapter, you will learn how to use these types and see how Go uses them to build a complex program.

Basic Types

The basic types are the most used types in every programming language. These types are the building blocks for the language and essentially the building blocks for more complex programs. The basic types are used to create variables:

- Strings

- Numerics

- Booleans

Numeric Types

Go defines three types of numeric types:

- Integers

- Floating-point numbers

- Complex

Each type has a specific signature and size for its value. So let's start with the integer. In Go, there are four sizes of integers:

- 8

- 16

- 32

- 64

All integer types can be *signed* or *unsigned*. A signed type of integer accepts values positive or negative; an unsigned type accepts only positive values.

You can define a signed type with the words int8, int16, int32, or int64, respectively, for integers of size 8, 16, 32, or 64 bits, respectively. If you want to define an unsigned type, you use the words uint8, uint16, uint32, or uint64. In Go, it is possible to define a number with the word int or uint as these two generic types define a signed or not-signed integer of at least 32 bits. The size of the number can be calculated in this range: -2^n to $2^{n-1}-1$ for the signed number and from 0 to 2^{n-1} for the unsigned number.

For instance, the range for an int16 is -32768 to 32767. The unsigned range is from 0 to 65538. It is possible declare a type of int with this basic syntax:

```
var ui uint8= 256
var  I int8 = 240
```

A floating-point number is another important type, in particular for the math operation in Go. You can define two types of float:

- float32

- float64

The floating-point number in Go is based on the standard IEEE 754. This standard is implemented in all new CPUs.

The limit of the floating-point number is huge and you can find it in the math package. The code in Listing 3-11 shows the maximum size for the float number.

Listing 3-11. Checking the Maximum Value for the Floating-Point Number in Go

```
package main

import (
"fmt"
"math"
)

func main() {
fmt.Println(math.MaxFloat32)
fmt.Println(math.MaxFloat64)
}
```

The result shown below is the max size of the floating-point number:

```
piggi@piggi:~/Desktop/HCL_Book/code/chapter_3$ go run number.go
3.4028234663852886e+38
1.7976931348623157e+308
```

It is possible to create a floating-point number with this syntax:

```
var f float32 = 12.323
var f64 float64 = 12.343549
```

Go has another type of number called the *complex number.* This type of number is built with a real part plus an imaginary part. In Go, you can define two types of complex numbers:

- complex64

- complex128

A complex number is essentially a floating point type but with an imaginary part plus a real part. To create a complex number, the same syntax is used to create a variable but with the word `complex`:

```
var com complex64 = complex(2, 3)
```

This creates a complex number composing of a real part (2) and an imaginary part (3).

A complex number is a number that can be expressed with the formula a + bi, where a and b are real numbers and i is the solution for the equation x^2 = -1. This number always has a real part and an imaginary part. The complex number is used in geometry, physics, and in applied mathematics, for example.

To isolate the real part and the imaginary part of the complex number, use the functions `real` and `imag` from the `math` library.

Booleans

A Boolean, defined as type `bool`, has only two possible values: `true` and `false`. `bool` is mostly used to check the condition of an `if` or `for` statement. To declare a `bool`:

```
var b bool = false
```

Go does not have an explicit function to convert the Boolean value into a number, so if you want one, you need to write one. See Listing 3-12.

Listing 3-12. The Go Program to Convert a bool into a Number

```
package main

import (
    "fmt"
)
```

```go
func boolConvertion(value bool) int {
    if value {
        return 1
    }

    return 0
}
func main() {
    fmt.Println(boolConvertion(true))
    fmt.Println(boolConvertion(false))
}
```

The function boolConvertion(value bool) converts the bool value into a number 1 or 0.

Strings

In Go, a string is an immutable sequence of characters. A string can contain any type of character with respect to the UTF-8 standard arbitrary length. A string is a sequence of human-readable characters.

The length of the string can be obtained by the function len. If you want to obtain the single character from a string, you can use [..] with the number of the position in the string. For example, s[1] gives you the character in position 1. Note that the length starts from the position 0. A string can be defined as follows:

```go
s:="Hello World"
```

The above represents a string s with the value "Hello World". Because a string is a sequence of characters, it is possible to slice the string get a substring. So if you want to get the characters 3 and 4 of the string s, you can write something like s[3:4], which will provide the substring from index 3 to 4, which is a single character in this example. See Listing 3-13.

Listing 3-13. Selecting a Character from a String

```go
package main

import (
"fmt"
)
```

```
func main() {
s := "Hello HCL"

fmt.Println(s[3:])   (1)
fmt.Println(s[:5])   (2)
fmt.Println(s[3:4]) (3)
}
```

This code selects all the characters from index 3 to the end: (1), from the start to index 5 (2), and the index character from position 3 to 4 (3). The result is shown in Listing 3-14.

Listing 3-14. The Result of the Program in Listing 3-13

```
piggi@piggi:$ go run string_selection.go
lo HCL
Hello
l
```

Strings are common in every programming language. Later in the book you will see how to manipulate and use them.

Composite Types

A composite type combines different basic types. The composite types are

- Arrays
- Slices
- Maps
- Structs

Array and structs are fixed-size structures. This means when you define them, you can't change the size. Maps and slices are dynamic structures, so you can change the size of the structure after you have created it.

Arrays

In Go, an array is an immutable fixed-length sequence of a variable of the same type. The length can be from 0 to the max number defined during the declaration.

```
var first_array [3]int
```

The syntax above defines an array of `int` of 3 elements. It is possible to access every element of an array using the positional access. When you declare an array without defining the value, all the elements of the array are initialized to the default value for the datatype. The default value is 0 when we have numeric variable for the array or an empty string. A simple program can help you understand this concept. See Listing 3-15.

Listing 3-15. A Simple Usage of the Array

```go
package main

import (
    "fmt"
)

func main() {
    var first_array [3]int
    var second [3]string
    fmt.Println(first_array[0])
    fmt.Println(first_array[2])

    fmt.Println(second[0])
    fmt.Println(second[2])
}
```

The code shows how to use an array in Go. If you run it, you will get the default result of the array:

```
piggi@piggi: go run array_example.go
0
0

piggi@piggi:
```

The default value for the int is 0; for string, it is an empty string. It is possible to declare and assign the value of an array during the declaration:

```
var p [3]int = [3]int{3,4,8}
```

This line creates and assigns the value to the array. It is possible to create an array without specifying a direct length but this is generated when you assign the values to the array:

```
p := [...]int {3,4,5, 10, 12}
```

The size of the array is obtained using the function len. The length of the array can be used to read the array itself using a for loop. See Listing 3-16.

Listing 3-16. The Code Updated to Read the Array

```
package main

import (
    "fmt"
)

func main() {
    var first_array [3]int
    var second [3]string
    fmt.Println(first_array[0])
    fmt.Println(first_array[2])

    fmt.Println(second[0])
    fmt.Println(second[2])
    for i := 0; i <= len(first_array)-1; i++ {
        fmt.Println(first_array[i])
    }
}
```

The new code reads the array and prints out the value of the array. Because the array is base 0, you need to read len-1 since the index of the array is 0,1,2.

Slices

A slice is similar to an array but the size of the slice is variable. When you define a slice, you use this syntax: [ ]T where T is the type of the slice.

To create a slice with non-zero length, you use the keyword make. To define the type of slice and the type of the element in the slice, see Listing 3-17.

Listing 3-17. Simple Code for Creating a Slice

```go
package main

import (
    "fmt"
)

func main() {
    n := make([]int, 3)

    fmt.Println(len(n))
}
```

A slice is more powerful than an array because the size can be changed. When the element is added to the slice itself, as in Listing 3-17 (which shows how to create a basic slice), the result of the program is the length of the slice, which in this case is 3. You can append new elements on the slice to change the length of the slice; see Listing 3-18.

Listing 3-18. The Code to Append Elements to the Slice

```go
package main

import (
    "fmt"
)

func main() {
    n := make([]int, 3)
    n[0] = 1 (1)
    fmt.Println(len(n))
    n = append(n, 4) (2)
    fmt.Println(len(n))
}
```

Listing 3-18 shows how to append elements to the slice and how to update the value of a specific element of the slice. Line (1) changes the value at position 0 of the slice to 1. Line (2) shows how to append a new element on the slice. This is done using the word append. The parameters for the function are the slice and the element plus what you need to add.

Maps

In Go, maps are a structure used to associate a key K to a value V. All the keys for a map are of the same type, likewise the maps.

Similar to slices, an empty map can be created by the word make. In order to populate the map, you can then append as necessary, as shown in Listing 3-19.

Listing 3-19. The Code to Create and Manage a Map

```
package main

import "fmt"

func main() {

    m := make(map[string]int) (1)

    m["k1"] = 7 (2)
    m["k2"] = 13 (3)

    fmt.Println("map:", m)

    v1 := m["k1"]
    fmt.Println("v1: ", v1)

    fmt.Println("len:", len(m))

    delete(m, "k2") (4)
    fmt.Println("map:", m)
}
```

Listing 3-19 shows the basic operation you can execute in maps. Line (1) creates an empty map where the key is of type string and the value is of type int.

Lines (2) and (3) add basic values to the map for values associated with keys k1 and k2. Line (4) shows how to remove an element from the maps. This is done using the function delete, which accepts two parameters: the map and the key you want to remove.

Structs

A struct is an aggregate data type that is used to bring together zero or more named values with a type. A struct is commonly used to aggregate common values. An example is if you want to create a table like-structure in your code.

Normal usage of a struct is to aggregate and create a record to be used inside a program whose name is used to "call" the record and read the value, as in Listing 3-20.

Listing 3-20. Creating and Using a Struct

```
package main

import "fmt"

type person struct { (1)
    name string
    age  int
}

func main() {

    fmt.Println(person{"Bob", 20}) (2)

    fmt.Println(person{name: "Alice", age: 30}) (3)

}
```

Listing 3-20 shows how to create and use a struct. Line (1) creates and defines the structure and the named variables inside it. Lines (2) and (3) insert values into the struct, which shows the necessity of indicating the field and value of the variable.

Channels

Channels are used to provide synchronization and communication between goroutines. A *goroutine* is a function or a method that runs concurrently with another method or function; this is similar to a thread in another language.

Channels are used to synchronize the communication across the goroutine. The operator <- is used to specify the channel direction to *send* or *receive*. If the operator is not specified, the channel is *bidirectional,* which means it is possible to send or receive a value from the channel.

```
send_channel <- float64 (1)

<-chan int (2)

bi_directional Gotest (3)
```

Line (1) defines the channel used only to *send* float64 on the goroutine. Line (2) defines a channel used only to *receive* a value int from the goroutine. Finally, line (3) creates a *bidirectional* channel used to send and receive the value of type Gotest. A channel can be of two types:

- *Buffered*: The channel is created with a maximum size of elements.

- *Unbuffered*: The channel is created with no maximum size of elements

It is possible to create a new channel using the built-in function make, as in Listing 3-21.

Listing 3-21. A Channel Example

```
package main

import "fmt"

func main() {

    new_channel := make(chan string) (1)

    go func() { new_channel <- "ping" }() (2)

    msg := < - new_channel (3)
    fmt.Println(msg)
}
```

Listing 3-21 shows how to create and use a channel. In line (1) you define a new channel using the built-in function make. The channel is created with the word chan and the type string.

The line (2) creates a new function using the channel you just created and assigns the value ping to the channel. Finally, in line (3) the variable msg is populated with the value of the channel. It is important to notice where the operator <- is placed. In line (2) the operator is placed after the declaration of the channel. This means the value defined is sent to the channel. In line (3) the operator is written before the channel name, which means the channel receives from the value.

Interface

Interface types in Go are similar to those in any other language: they are used to define a signature of an object as a set of method.

Interfaces are defined using this syntax: *type <name of interface> interface {....}*. For example, you can define an interface as shown in Listing 3-22.

Listing 3-22. The Definition of a Go Interface

```
type math_function interface {
    addition()
    subtraction()
}
```

The interface math_function defines two methods named addition and subtraction, as shown in Listing 3-23.

Listing 3-23. Using an Interface in Go

```
package main

import (
    "fmt"
)

type math_function interface { (1)
    addition() int
    subtraction() int
}

type numbers struct {
    n1, n2 int
}
```

```
func (v numbers)addition() int { (2)
    return v.n1 + v.n2
}
func (v numbers)subtraction() int { (3)
    return v.n1 - v.n2
}

func operations(n math_function) { (4)
    fmt.Println(n)
    fmt.Println(n.addition())
    fmt.Println(n.subtraction())
}

func main() {
    v := numbers{n1: 6, n2: 4}

    operations(v)
}
```

Listing 3-23 shows how to use the interface in Go. Line (1) defines the interface called math_function, and this interface defines two methods, addition and subtraction. Lines (2) and (3) define a method for using the interface and line (4) defines a function to extend the interface. If you run the code, you get these results:

```
{6 4}
10
2
```

Functions

A function is an aggregation of commands to solve a specific functionality. This function has been used in all of our programs until now: func main(). The basic syntax for creating a function is

```
func <function name>(<parameters>) (<return type>){
 <body function>
}
```

A function is a piece of code that returns a value. If, for example, you want to create a function for getting the sum of two numbers, you can write

```go
func sum(a int, b int) int {

    return a + b
}
```

This function executes the sum of the numbers a and b and returns an int. You can use the function in this way:

```go
package main

import "fmt"

func sum(a int, b int) int {

    return a + b
}

func main() {

    res := sum(1, 2)
    fmt.Println("1+2 =", res)
}
```

The variable res calls the function and stores the returned value in a variable. You can then print the value and see the result.

Conditional Statements

Conditional statements if...then...else are used to check a code condition and change the execution of the code based on the condition. Go and if...then...else have the same structure as other languages. It is possible to create an if...then without an else and it is possible to have an if...then...else if.

```go
package main

import (
    "fmt"
)
```

```go
func main() {
    i := 1

    if i > 5 {
        fmt.Println("Hello")
    } else {
        fmt.Println("World")
    }
}
```

This code shows how to use the comparison operator to make a comparison between two values. The `if` can be declared without any `else`. This means if the condition of the `if` is not meet, the code inside the body is not executed.

Another conditional expression you can use is `switch`. It is used when you want to check a condition against multiple choices:

```go
i := 2
fmt.Print("The number  ", i, " is ")
switch i {
case 1:
    fmt.Println("one")
case 2:
    fmt.Println("two")
case 3:
    fmt.Println("three")
}
```

Conditional statements are extensively used. The Go conditional statement is similar to those used in other languages such as Java or C#.

Loop Conditions

Go supports only one loop constructor: the `for` statement. This constructor is used to repeat the same operation for a specific number of executions. The basic `for` loop is created with just one condition:

```
for c <= 3 {
    fmt.Println(c)
    c = c + 1
}
```

In the first example, the `for` loop is executed until the `c` is less than or equal to 3. The code increments the condition to make it finish. The second type of `for` loop is to define the condition to check and increment the `for` statement:

```
for j := 5; j <= 8; j++ {
    fmt.Println(j)
}
```

This is similar to other languages where the condition is the initial statement and the variable(s) are incremented in the same statement.

The last type of `for` loop is the infinite `for` loop. This type of `for` statement does not have any conditions to break the execution on its definition and normally breaks dependent on some other external condition. This type of loop is used, for example, when you need to read data from a network or when you create a web server:

```
for {
    fmt.Println("loop")
    break
}
```

The word `break` is used to terminate the `for` loop and then exit from the loop. Execution of the `for` loop can be continued using the expression `continue`.

Conclusion

This chapter was a short introduction to the Go programming language. The choice of Go for writing code is strictly connected with its flexibility. Understanding the basics of the language is extremely important for the rest of the book. The remaining chapters will show you how to use Go to build Infrastructure as Code in conjunction with HashiCorp.

CHAPTER 4

Infrastructure as Code

Infrastructure as Code (IaC) has become an integral part of various careers in ICT, particularly in relation to the cloud. Software like Kubernetes, Docker, Chef, and Puppet lead the charge in utilizing IaC in daily operations. The HashiCorp suite fits perfectly into this genre. Tools like Terraform, Vault, and Vagrant can be used to create fully automated environments for realizing automation. In this chapter, we will introduce the basic principles of Infrastructure as Code from a theoretical perspective. This is fundamental for better design and implementing the automation in real applications.

Introduction to Infrastructure as Code

If we want to define IaC, this line could articulate it: *"Infrastructure as Code, IaC, is the process to manage and provision computer via machine-readable code."*

IaC has grown in tandem with the growth in popularity of the cloud. For instance, for IaaS (Infrastructure as a Service), Infrastructure as Code supports IaaS but is actually separate from it.

Infrastructure as a Service is one of the four types of the cloud defined by the NIST document 800-145. This type of cloud has the capacity to provision storage, network capability, processing, and another fundamental computing resource. These resources can be used to run arbitrary software like operating systems and software created ad-hoc.

Infrastructure as Code has the following three advantages:

- Cost reduction
- Faster execution when you release the infrastructure
- Reducing errors during the release of the infrastructure

65

© Pierluigi Riti and David Flynn 2021
P. Riti and D. Flynn, *Beginning HCL Programming*, https://doi.org/10.1007/978-1-4842-6634-2_4

The first aspect we can improve with IaC is *cost reduction.* IaC reduces costs by defining the infrastructure in a file. This essentially allows us to generate in the same hardware, the definition of a different architecture and infrastructure combination without needing to buy new hardware any time. It can then be released automatically. In case of a challenge, you can roll back to a previous configuration. Without this facility and specific software, the engineer would have to spend days or even weeks to release the infrastructure, create the VM, and configure it, all of which can be negated by using IaC. The software for IaC can be released in a matter of hours, creating new infrastructure. This capability can lead to faster execution. Since the IaC is released by the computer, this manifests the advantage of *reducing errors during the release.*

IaC for your infrastructure usually essentially involves writing a file that defines the infrastructure. This can in turn be included in a CI/CD cycle, followed by a test stage plus code review. This drives an uptick in the quality of the code and potentially reduces errors during the release of the infrastructure.

Principles and Goals for IaC

When a company decides to embark on a journey to implement IaC, obviously some changes to smooth the transition are necessary to achieve this goal. The following team procedures or changes to mindsets and mantras are usually necessary:

- Support or change in the IT infrastructure becomes the norm and is not seen as an obstacle.

- Making a change to the system is a routine, not a problem.

- The release becomes a simple and repetitive task, and allows the engineer responsible for the decommissioning of the infrastructure to do some more important tasks.

- The technical team is able to define and release its own infrastructure.

- The infrastructure can be easily rolled back in case there is an issue.

- The infrastructure follows the principle of CI/CD, which means the infrastructure is released continuously in small pieces and not in one big release.

The adoption of IaC requires the following principles:

- Every system must be reproducible.

- Every system must be disposable.

- Every system must be consistent.

- Every system must be repeatable.

- The design of the system always changes.

These principles are the basis on which you can build your IaC project. We will briefly describe these principles so you can better understand how to put them in place and how they help your IaC process.

Every System Must Be Reproducible

To facilitate good IaC, the entire infrastructure must be robust enough to spin up and down within a certain time frame all of the infrastructure, or a small piece of it.

Because the system is defined in a machine-readable file, the infrastructure can be easily installed multiple times. All details about hostname, network name, etc. should be in the configuration file used for the IaC in order to allow for easy repetition.

Every System Must Be Disposable

When we talk about IaC, we imply dynamism in that all facets of the infrastructure such as resize, removal, etc. can be effected.

These changes cannot influence the correct functionality of the infrastructure. The infrastructure must be reliable and consistent across all changes. It becomes particularly important to have a dynamic infrastructure that can be easily disposed of in case of failure without creating an issue for other infrastructural modules.

Every System Must Be Consistent

When a system is created using IaC, it is essential, for example, that two servers configured with the same script are the same. The only difference can be the IP address or the server name.

This principle prevents inconsistency such as when we create a server in GCP or AWS. We define the server using a template; this template is used for defining the size of the HDD, the number of CPUs, etc. This consistency is important in order to avoid disruption of the services.

Every System Must Be Repeatable

The core principle of IaC is to have a repeatable process. It is very important to apply the other principles of IaC.

When we define an IaC file, we need to define a file that can be repeated and the result must be identical for every run execution. If the process is not repeatable, as in changes manifest during execution, we will have instability.

The Design of the System Always Changes

With a conventional infrastructure, all changes incur unnecessary cost overruns plus delays. Due to the nature of IT, no one can foresee how frequently changes will need to be made to the infrastructure. IaC, especially in conjunction with a cloud environment, can result in faster turnarounds. Automation with proven configurations tested in lower environments enforces this.

Implementing IaC

For a successfully implement IaC, a defined process needs to be followed.

The cornerstone of IaC is the *definition file*. The definition file is used to define every single piece of the infrastructure such as servers, databases, networks, etc. Various tools such as Chef, Ansible, or Terraform written in a common DSL language facilitate this. See Listing 4-1.

Listing 4-1. An Example Terraform Definition File

```
resource "aws_instance" "hcl_example" {
 ami                = "ami-21f78e11"
 availability_zone = "us-east-1"
 instance_type     = "a1.medium"
```

```
  tags {
    Name = "HCL-EC2"
  }
}
resource "aws_ebs_volume" "ebs_volume" {
 availability_zone = "$us-east-1"
 size              = 1

   tags {
     Name = "EBS-volume"
   }
}
resource "aws_volume_attachment" "hcl_vol_attachment" {
 device_name = "/dev/sdh"
 volume_id   = aws_ebs_volume.ebs_volume.id
 instance_id = aws_instance.hcl_example.id
}
```

Listing 4-1 presents a piece of a configuration file from Terraform. A *resource* is defined, in this case as an AWS instance. The code defines all of the information needed for the instance using *tags*. This code organization helps you isolate different pieces of infrastructure and makes versioning simpler.

Defining infrastructure in a file helps create documentation for the project. Documentation can be easily extracted from the definition file. This also greatly enables testing.

Automatic code release means human interaction is reduced or totally absent, in this context allowing for continuous testing. Another advantage of IaC is that large changes can be broken down into smaller pieces, reducing downtime. Reliability and security are also improved since a small, continuous process produces fast feedback or results. This feedback in turn enhances quality since a quick rollback is possible in case of errors or bugs. See Figure 4-1.

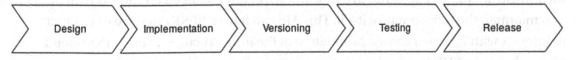

Figure 4-1. *Phases for IaC*

Dynamic Infrastructure and the Cloud

A *dynamic infrastructure* is a platform that provides computing resources such as memory, disk space, or network resources that can be programmatically defined.

Reading this definition, you can easily visualize the cloud and dynamic infrastructure as quick collaborators. Good examples are public IaaS such as AWS or GCP.

Not only does the public cloud allow the creation of a dynamic infrastructure, but this dynamic infrastructure can be created using software for virtualization, namely OpenStack.

Any dynamic infrastructure must have some specific characteristics:

- Must be programmable

- Must be on-demand

- Must be self-service

Analyzing these characteristics, we find a striking similarity with the NIST definition of the cloud. Dynamic infrastructure can be defined as a small cloud. The NIST defines the cloud as

- On-demand and self-service

- Broad network access

- Resource pooling

- Rapid elasticity

- Measured service

In a dynamic infrastructure, resource pooling is not immediately apparent or necessary. However, the sharing of infrastructure across different users or business units is a natural evolution.

The first characteristic of the dynamic infrastructure is the programmability of the infrastructure. To define the dynamic infrastructure, we need an API to create and maintain the infrastructure itself. This API can have a REST interface or another to interact with it, which allows the creation of the infrastructure. Every public cloud normally has an SDK that facilitates interaction to define and create the infrastructure programmatically. Another important characteristic for dynamic infrastructure is that the infrastructure must to be *on-demand.* Essentially this means we can destroy the infrastructure as needed, which is important from a budgetary and flexibility point of view.

Connected with on-demand is *self-service.* This capability allows the infrastructure to alter itself. This capability allows the user to improve the infrastructure or define the infrastructure based on its necessity. A user must to be able to design the infrastructure based on their specific needs. For example, a user may need more storage than most. This self-service capability is important in order to have a successful adoption of the dynamic infrastructure across the different business units.

Different Types of Dynamic Infrastructures

There are different types of dynamic infrastructures. It is important to understand the different types and definitions to better identify what is best for the current project and what is prudent from a business sense. As stated, the definition of a dynamic infrastructure is essentially similar to the cloud definition. There are three main definitions:

1. *SaaS, Software as a Service*: This is software shared across different users. An example of SaaS is Gmail or Office365.

2. *PaaS, Platform as a Service*: This is a platform used to create software and hence to develop and host the software.

3. *IaaS, Infrastructure as a Service: This is a platform for creating a basic infrastructure.*

A dynamic infrastructure is essentially IaaS. The definition and functionality for IaaS is used to define the basic infrastructure of the system, which in turn allows for the creation of software based on said infrastructure. IaaS can be *private* or *public;* the difference is the level of access. In a *private IaaS,* the provider allows the user to build it all from scratch. The provider offers the basic components and the user builds their own infrastructure. Examples of IaaS are Google Cloud, AWS, and Azure.

An important decision about the dynamic infrastructure is the business case for private or public cloud infrastructure.

The first consideration is the security of the data. The security of the data is different for a public infrastructure versus a public infrastructure. Concerns mostly revolve around the type of data and its corresponding legislation. In a public cloud infrastructure, the data center is not inside the company and therefore we have no control over the data. We do not know who has access to the data and we don't know the level of security for the data. Conversely, in a private infrastructure, we retain full control of the data and access is restricted due to our control of physical security. One possible solution is to have a hybrid solution. In this configuration, it is possible to maintain the data inside the company and have in the public infrastructure only the OS and the network management segments.

Another consideration to make is scalability relative to necessity. With a public infrastructure, it is easy to scale the infrastructure up and down and pay only for what is needed. This is important when the system needs to address a huge number of requests connected with a specific momentary event.

The last point to consider is the cost of the infrastructure and the total cost of the operation. A private infrastructure can have higher costs than a public infrastructure. The expense to consider is not only connected with the cost of the initial hosting but also ongoing maintenance.

Tools for IaC

To design and maintain IaC, it is important to have the right tools. There are a wide range of tools available. It usually comes down to familiarity. The options generally boil down to software like Cloud Formation, Openstack, or Terraform.

All Infrastructure as Code processes are based on the automation principles described earlier in the chapter. Some basic requirements are

1. Scriptable interface

2. Support for the CLI (command line interface)

3. Must be reliable

4. Must have an external configuration file

The first requirement of a good tool is to have a scriptable interface. To enable full automation, the tool must be configured via code using an API or the internal CLI. For example, in Terraform it is possible to use HCL to define the infrastructure, allowing the smooth creation of the actual configuration.

The first requirement drives the second and third requirements. In terms of support for the CLI, for faster maintenance the CLI allows the system administrator to execute commands directly on the infrastructure created. Rapid changes can also be facilitated through the CLI.

The third requirement, reliability, in this context refers to consistent results performed by the script on each iteration. To achieve this requirement, some scripts characteristics can be defined:

1. *Reliable*: The script must return the same result any time we execute with the same value. This is important for building trust.

2. *Input and output check:* The script must check the output for each input. If there is an issue with the result, then it must return a clear message to the user. This lends itself to better security and maintenace.

3. *Clear failure*: The script must have a clear condition in case of an error. This is important for having a clear status about the code and for understanding what's happening when the code is running.

4. *Parameterized:* The script must be able to accept some parameter or argument to configure an execution, such configuring the path for the log or the user executing the process.

These characteristics are not new for developers but are a new concept for some system administrators. These characteristics help you write a good and stable script for Infrastructure as Code.

Defining IaC

The main component of Infrastructure as Code is the *definition file.* The definition file is used to create and maintain the infrastructure. The scope of the definition file is to describe what type of infrastructure you want to build and its parameters. The format for a definition file is a text file, such as a Vault definition file. See Listing 4-2.

Listing 4-2. The Vault Definition File

```
storage "consul" { (1)
  address = "127.0.0.1:8500"
  path    = "vault"
}

listener "tcp" { (2)
  address     = "127.0.0.1:8200"
  tls_disable = 1
}

telemetry { (3)
  statsite_address = "127.0.0.1:8125"
  disable_hostname = true
}
```

If you analyze this configuration file, it is possible to identify the basic characteristic of the definition file: sections (1), (2), and (3) define the basic components for the infrastructure. In this case, it's `storage`, `listener`, and `telemetry`.

Every section has the value for the specific component of the infrastructure to configure. So, if you analyze the first section,

```
storage "consul" {
  address = "127.0.0.1:8500"
  path    = "vault"
}
```

it is possible to see the `address` and `path`. The address is the IP address for the server, and where is stored the data is the path.

A definition file has another advantage in that the file is auto-documented. This is essential in order to better understand what the file does.

Releasing IaC

It is necessary to adopt some engineering practices to realize better maintenance of the infrastructure. It is possible to identify some basic patterns for the different sections of the definition file. These patterns can be split into the following different phases:

1. Provisioning

2. Management

3. Updating

4. Definition

These four phases are needed to implement Infrastructure as Code. *Provisioning* is the process of building an element of infrastructure such as a server. The provisioning is one of the basic processes of Infrastructure as Code. To be effective, provisioning must respect some characteristics:

1. On-demand

2. Define once

3. Transparent

On-demand means the infrastructure can be easily rebuilt without undue effort. The infrastructure can be executed and deployed without any constraints. *Define once* specifies that every element in IaC must be defined once and then can be rebuilt n-time(s) as needed to design the infrastructure. This characteristic is important because in case of error we can easily rebuild the entire infrastructure multiple times without changing the result of the operation. *Transparent* is the requirement that each element in the definition file must be easy to read and modify.

Management is the process for managing and maintaining the servers. This process also involves the process for saving and versioning the definition file.

Update is the creation of a new piece of software or updating the existing infrastructure with a new version for the OS, for instance.

One of the most important changes driven by Infrastructure as Code is to enable the continuous release of the infrastructure. The release of the infrastructure is used mostly to synchronize the infrastructure, correcting its state. There are essentially two patterns for synchronizing the infrastructure:

1. *Pushing the change*

2. *Pulling the change*

These two patterns are used to apply the changes in the infrastructure. The main difference between these two patterns is who initiates the change. With the *pushing pattern*, there is a central node that manages the changes and pushes the scheduled times. For example, every 20 minutes the central software node pushes the changes to the clients connected to that node. With the *pulling pattern*, the client checks with the central server if there is a change to receive.

Pushing vs. Pulling

Pushing and pulling are two methods used to update and install the new infrastructure. There are pros and cons to both methods.

Push uses a central management server to *push* the changes to the client. This configuration requires a client running on all nodes. The client receives the configuration to apply on the host.

The client normally communicates with the server using an SSH channel. Ansible uses the SSH daemon in conjunction with Python.

The advantage of push is having a centralized server to push the configuration for the infrastructure. One disadvantage is in the architecture design since to effectively design a loosely coupled architecture, it is important to reduce dependencies.

In comparison, the *pull method has an agent on each host* which at a specific time checks for a configuration from a central repository. One of the advantages is security. This method requires the host to connect to a central system. This helps with security concerns because the central system talks with the client via just one port and one user. In the push pattern, the system can have more than one user and port to configure and thus much more to secure.

Deciding whether to use a push or pull system requires an understanding of the underlying architecture. A pull-based system is more scalable than a push-based system. This depends on the configuration of the system. A pull-based system doesn't rely on only one node to pull down the configuration. This means it is possible to add a number of nodes and scale the architecture.

On the other hand, the push system has a central node to manage the nodes. It is not really possible to scale up the architecture compared with a pull system. To scale up the push system, the design needs more than one central node. This means having different parts of the infrastructure, such as getting the configuration from a different server location. This can be, for example, a split based on the geographical area, but this means we need to be sure all of the central nodes have exactly the same configuration. However, this increases the complexity and requires more resources of the push system.

Engineering Practices for IaC

The central caveat behind Infrastructure as Code is to utilize the same principles used for software engineering. The main focus of a software engineer practice is to enhance the quality of the system. This is done following these practices and principles:

1. To delivery working code at an early stage

2. To delivery said code in a continuous manner

3. To build code of a high quality

4. To build a small piece of code at every iteration in a continuous cycle

5. To ensure that each release achieves the highest quality

6. To obtain constructive feedback for every release

7. To expect change

These principles are inspired by the Agile Manifesto, which drives change and hence the development of Infrastructure as Code. Applying these principles in your IaC development helps you introduce and develop high quality code. The main focus is to improve the quality of the system.

Improving the System Quality

One of the most important engineering principles is system quality. Having good quality is key to having a system that is maintainable and scalable.

To build the quality on your system, it is necessary to put in place some practices in your development life cycle:

1. Use version control.

2. Unit test the code.

3. Build a CI.

4. Comment the code.

These practices are common for software development. In IaC, the quality is improved, which makes the system more stable and easy to scale or maintain. It is easy to commit this practice to the IaC definition since IaC is defined using a file.

Quality of software is not only concerned with the expected response of functions but also with the capacity to maintain code, comment the code, and unit test the code. All of this helps maintain the code for changes or maintenance.

To enhance overall quality in the system, all of practices listed above must be utilized at each iteration. The result is to enable fast feedback on each iteration to analyze whether your infrastructure is stable and reliable.

Version control is important (versioning the infrastructure) because the system is a text file. It is easy to version this file in a source control like Git. To have a file under version control enables another engineer to perform a code review. This improves the quality of code and it also disseminates knowledge of the code, inducing a positive discussion.

Conclusion

This chapter introduced Infrastructure as Code, which is essentially a way to create infrastructure using the software development cycle. This achieves a faster and better quality system. IaC is quickly becoming more important, particularly in conjunction with the cloud. HashiCorp software is enabling this revolution by maximizing quality with increased efficiency when build an infrastructure.

## CHAPTER 5

Terraform HCL

Terraform is the de facto standard technique for cloud and Infrastructure as Code. Terraform is a tool for building, maintaining, and releasing IaC in a wide range of *providers.* In this chapter, you will learn what Terraform is and how to use it in the cloud and transform your DevOps journey.

The DevOps and Cloud Revolution

No so long ago, releasing software was a long and painful process. After the development phase, there was the release phase. The release engineer could spend sometimes weeks performing installs to make the software work properly. When the software was eventually released, ongoing maintenance would or could require ongoing interactions between the dev and release teams. This process was cumbersome, entailing interactions revolving around bug identification and fixes.

Software was, or still is, released on physical hardware. This creates other challenges concerning the scalability of the software itself. The hardware normally is a little "overpowered" in order to accommodate an increase in traffic.

In 2008 at the Toronto Agile Conference, Patrick Debois did a presentation called "Agile Infrastructure and Operations." Debois presented evidence about the difference between the developer and the operational engineer during the SDLC (software-defined life cycle). The idea behind the talk was to make the developer more responsible for the software itself and to remove the gap between the developer and the operational engineer.

In 2009, Patrick Debois created the first DevOpsDays conference and coined the term *DevOps.* DevOps is now a buzzword in IT, and companies are adopting this methodology every day.

With DevOps, the company not only changes the way it works across the team but completely changes the mentality around the software development release. DevOps

© Pierluigi Riti and David Flynn 2021
P. Riti and D. Flynn, *Beginning HCL Programming*, https://doi.org/10.1007/978-1-4842-6634-2_5

changes the way how the company releases the entire software, reducing time-to-market. This is possible because the DevOps methodology is built on these pillars:

- Continuous integration (CI)

- Continuous delivery (CD)

- Agile methodologies

- Infrastructure as Code

This discipline requires a change not only in technology but also how the team manages the workload.

In order for DevOps to be effective, the barriers across the different company departments need to be brought down so all departments can collaborate more effectively. When the software engineer designs the software, they must keep in mind the maintainability of the software itself to meet best practices.

Another important improvement of DevOps is to reduce the failure during the release because the CI/CD practice releases small pieces of software, such as the change of just a label. Because the software is versioned, it's easy redeploy the original code if necessary.

The DevOps methodologies really work well with the cloud. When a company decides to move the software to a cloud environment such as AWS, GCP, and Azure, deployment is sped up and this process becomes easier. This is encouraged by the fact that the cloud supports IaC more effectively.

DevOps in combination with the cloud is now a must-know for every software engineer. The DevOps is a complete change of the culture, which can be summarized with four words: *culture, automation, measurement,* and *sharing.* To be effective, the DevOps team needs to embrace the changes behind this statement. In the rest of the book, we will focus on only *automation.* This is where the HashiCorp suite is perfectly suited for automation, which covers every area of the SLDC.

IaC in Practice

Terraform is the de facto standard when discussing Infrastructure as Code. IaC was born with this idea of creating and executing code that can be used to define, deploy, and maintain the entire infrastructure.

Automation can start with a simple script. Imagine a basic bash script used to "create" the server after installation. A script to download and untar Tomcat is similar to the concept in Listing 5-1.

Listing 5-1. A Simple Script for Downloading and Untaring the Tomcat File

```
# Update the software
sudo apt update
sudo apt install default-JDK
# Create the user
sudo groupadd tomcat
# Add the user to the group
sudo useradd -s /bin/false -g tomcat -d /opt/tomcat tomcat
# Move on the /tmp folder
cd /tmp
# Download the Tomcat file
curl -O https://www-eu.apache.org/dist/tomcat/tomcat-9/v9.0.30/bin/apache-
tomcat-9.0.30.tar.gz
# Install Tomcat on the /opt folder
sudo mkdir /opt/tomcat
sudo tar xzvf apache-tomcat-9*tar.gz -C /opt/tomcat –strip-components=1
```

The simple script in Listing 5-1 is used to download and untar the Tomcat software in the machine. Such a script is one of thousands used every day by SysAdmins to automate the process of creating and configuring a new server. This script could be used in a suite of other scripts to create and configure such a server. The script is essentially a general purpose script and can be written in any language. In this example, Bash is used but it's possible to use Python.

Using a general purpose language can be easy at the start but at the same time it can be complex. The script can be easy if you need to configure one specific environment but imagine if you need to configure the environment in a different cloud provider such as AWS or GCP, or with a different virtualization provider such as VirtualBox/VMWare.

The *configuration management tools* are a family of software used to describe the configuration you want to apply on the system. Software from this family includes Puppet, Chef, and Ansible.

For example, if you want to translate in Chef the same code you used to install Tomcat, see Listing 5-2.

Listing 5-2. The Chef Recipe for Installing and Configuring Tomcat

```
# make sure we have java installed
include_recipe 'java'

user 'tomcat'

# put tomcat in the group so we can make sure we don't remove it by
managing cool_group
group 'cool_group' do
members 'tomcat'
action :create
end

# Install Tomcat 8.0.47 to the default location
tomcat_install 'helloworld' do tarball_uri 'http://archive.apache.org/dist/
tomcat/tomcat-8/v8.0.47/bin/ap
     ache-tomcat-8.0.47.tar.gz'
     tomcat_user 'cool_user'
     tomcat_group 'cool_group'
end

# Install Tomcat 8.0.47 to the default location mode 0755
tomcat_install 'dirworld' do
     dir_mode '0755'
     tarball_uri 'http://archive.apache.org/dist/tomcat/tomcat-8/v8.0.47/
     bin/ap
     ache-tomcat-8.0.47.tar.gz'
     tomcat_user 'cool_user'
     tomcat_group 'cool_group'
end

# Drop off our own server.xml that uses a non-default port setup
     cookbook_file '/opt/tomcat_helloworld/conf/server.xml' do
     source 'helloworld_server.xml'
     owner 'root'
     group 'root'
     mode '0644'
```

```
      notifies :restart, 'tomcat_service[helloworld]'
end

remote_file '/opt/tomcat_helloworld/webapps/sample.war' do
    owner 'cool_user'
    mode '0644'
    source 'https://tomcat.apache.org/tomcat-6.0-doc/appdev/sample/sample.
    war'
    checksum
    '89b33caa5bf4cfd235f060c396cb1a5acb2734a1366db325676f48c5 f5ed9 2e5'
end

# start the helloworld tomcat service using a non-standard pic location
    tomcat_service 'helloworld' do
    action [:start, :enable]
    env_vars [{ 'CATALINA_BASE' =>
    '/opt/tomcat_helloworld/' }, { 'CATALINA_PID' =>
    '/opt/tomcat_helloworld/bin/non_standard_location.pid' },
    { 'SOMETHING' => 'some_value' }]
    sensitive true
    tomcat_user 'cool_user'
    tomcat_group 'cool_group'
end
```

The script looks longer compared to what you had initially, but there are some big differences. The first one is that the script correctly configures all the users and the group for Tomcat. Two, the script does not have any reference to a specific system. This means the script can be run in every system with the Chef client installed.

With Bash, you can reproduce the same script for your system, but using a configuration management tool offers some advantages:

- *Code conventions*: Every configuration management tool has its own language. In Chef, there is a DSL directly derived from Ruby. This convention forces you to use the convention and the rules defined for the configuration management. This is used to help better manage the code itself.

- *Reusability*: Configuration management normally uses a client for connecting to the server. Because you have a client and normally a DSL language, the same script can be reused in the different platforms without any need of a change.

- *Use for multiple servers*: A script for a configuration management tool is not perceived for a single server but is designed and developed to be executed on hundreds of servers. The same script can be executed in different environments such as a development server, a staging server, and a production server. Any script modification usually revolves around a parameter change.

The technique described until now essentially uses a configuration management tool to configure the server. This means the software is installed on the server and every time something changes; the software is realigned with the server to have exactly the same configuration.

Another technique alternative to the configuration management tool is called a templating tools. Software like Packer, Docker, or Vagrant is used to create an image of the server and is then release to all servers in one shot.

The image contains all the software, users, and configuration necessary to make the server fully operational. The image can then be released all at once, which facilitates a faster release of the system itself. Since the image is versioned, it is possible to do a rollback to a previous version in minutes. The image can then be managed and released using any other IaC software such as Ansible that is able to release an image on a system. There are two major categories of tools that run an image:

- *Virtual machines*: Software like Vagrant uses a virtual machine to emulate the operating system. What you run is a hypervisor, which is used to define and emulate the hardware used to run the application.

- *Containers*: They don't emulate all of the operating system, only the user space of an operating system. The container runs normally in a container engine like Docker or CoreOS rkt. This software is used to create an isolated environment for the user space. The big difference between virtual machines and containers is that the container can just see the user space on the container engine. It does not share any hardware configuration with the underlying operating system.

When you define a container for your IaC, you need the concept of the immutable infrastructure. This concept is achieved because every time you need to release or update the infrastructure with the container, you essentially release a completely new infrastructure. A container never updates the infrastructure, but every simple change requires a completely new release of the infrastructure itself.

Terraform for Server Provisioning

Configuration management tools and templating tools offer ways to configuring a server but for a complete IaC it is important to use a server provisioning tool such as Terraform or Cloudform.

A server provisioning tool is essential for creating the server itself. With this tool, you do not create only the server but also the load balancer, database, firewall, and IAM policy plus every other aspect connected with the server creation. The sequence diagram for a server provisioning tool is shown in Figure 5-1.

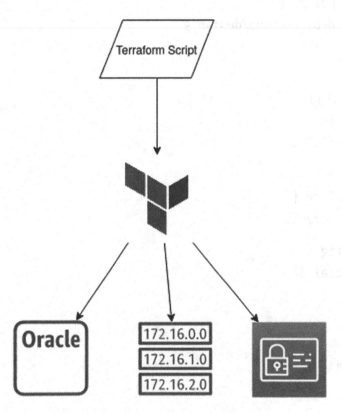

Figure 5-1. *The Terraform server provisioning workflow*

Figure 5-1 shows the basic workflow for server provisioning with Terraform. It is possible to provide all of the configuration necessary for the server, for example, the database, the IP table, and the Identity Access Management.

Terraform uses the HCL to define the configuration you want to provision on the server. Listing 5-3 shows an example of a Terraform file for configuring a GCP instance.

Listing 5-3. The Terraform Configuration for Writing a GCP Basic Instance

```
resource "google_compute_instance" "default" {
  name          = "test"
  machine_type = "n1-standard-1"
  zone          = "us-central1-a"

  tags = ["foo", "bar"]

  boot_disk {
    initialize_params {
      image = "debian-cloud/debian-9"
    }
  }

  // Local SSD disk
  scratch_disk {
    interface = "SCSI"
  }

  network_interface {
    network = "default"

    access_config {
      // Ephemeral IP
    }
  }

  metadata = {
    foo = "bar"
  }

  metadata_startup_script = "echo hi > /test.txt"
```

```
service_account {
    scopes = ["userinfo-email", "compute-ro", "storage-ro"]
  }
}
```

We will analyze the syntax later in the chapter but for now it is important to observe how with Terraform you can define a resource. A resource is essentially a piece of architecture you need to deploy for your IaC. In this case, you create a new Debian instance. The instance is very simple and is used to configure the default network and connect a basic hard disk for the storage.

Starting with Terraform

In Chapter 1, you installed Terraform and got a basic introduction. It is now time to get your hands dirty to get a better understanding of Terraform.

It is possible to use another feature offered by HashiCorp, the Terraform Cloud, at `https://app.terraform.io/session`. Terraform Cloud is free for small teams and can be used to test the HCL script in Terraform in a collaborative way.

Terraform can be used in a wide range of clouds, both public and private. In the example, we have provided AWS due to its popularity. The next step is to create the AWS account you need to test the code.

To connect Terraform with your AWS instance, you need to use your AWS credentials. First, check if Terraform is actually configured. To confirm this, open a command line and write `terraform`. The result should be similar to Listing 5-4.

Listing 5-4. The Terraform Command Line

```
Usage: terraform [-version] [-help] <command> [args]

The available commands for execution are listed below.
The most common, useful commands are shown first, followed by
less common or more advanced commands. If you're just getting
started with Terraform, stick with the common commands. For the other
commands, please read the help and docs before usage.
```

Common commands:
```
    apply               Builds or changes infrastructure
    console             Interactive console for Terraform interpolations
    destroy             Destroy Terraform-managed infrastructure
    env                 Workspace management
    fmt                 Rewrites config files to canonical format
    get                 Download and install modules for the configuration
    graph               Create a visual graph of Terraform resources
    import              Import existing infrastructure into Terraform
    init                Initialize a Terraform working directory
    output              Read an output from a state file
    plan                Generate and show an execution plan
    providers         Prints a tree of the providers used in the configuration
    refresh             Update local state file against real resources
    show                Inspect Terraform state or plan
    taint               Manually mark a resource for recreation
    untaint             Manually unmark a resource as tainted
    validate            Validates the Terraform files
    version             Prints the Terraform version
    workspace           Workspace management
```

All other commands:
```
    0.12upgrade         Rewrites pre-0.12 module source code for v0.12
    debug               Debug output management (experimental)
    force-unlock        Manually unlock the terraform state
    push              Obsolete command for Terraform Enterprise legacy (v1)
    state               Advanced state management
```

Now you need to export your access key to the AWS environment. In a Linux/Unix system, it is possible to use the export command to do that, so add to the .bashrc file the following lines:

```
export AWS_ACCESS_KEY_ID=<key id>
export AWS_SECRET_ACCESS_KEY=<secret key>
```

To reload the `.bashrc`, use the command `source .bashrc`. This creates the variable in your environment and allows Terraform to connect with your AWS environment.

Deploying Your First Server

With the environment finally ready, you can create your first deployment. Terraform uses the HCL language to create the deployment file necessary for the release of your Infrastructure as Code. This file is a simple text file with the extension `.tf` because it is a text file. It is possible to write the file with any editor like Notepad, Sublime, Vi, or Vim.

Writing a Terraform file requires some specific steps. The first one is to define the provider you want to use; in your case, it is AWS. The provider is defined in the main file which is called `main.tf`; see Listing 5-5.

Listing 5-5. The Terraform File main.tf

```
provider "aws" {
  region = "us-east-1"
}
```

We used the region "us-east-1" because this is the default of our AWS account. This can be different depending on where you open the AWS account.

The `main.tf` file creates a new provider AWS. The provider is used to identify where you deploy your infrastructure. The only value you add in this case is the region; our infrastructure is in the region: "us-east-1".

Every provider has a different resource. The resource is used to define all of the functionality of the infrastructure you want to define. For example, to define what VPS you want to use, see the code in Listing 5-6.

Listing 5-6. The main.tf with the VPC Defined

```
provider "aws" {
  region = "us-east-1"
}

# Create a VPC
resource "aws_vpc" "hclbookvpc" {
  cidr_block = "20.0.0.0/16"
}
```

To define a resource in HCL, you need to respect a specific syntax. The general syntax is

```
resource RESOURCE_TYPE, NAME{
    CONFIGURATION PARAMETERS
}
```

The RESOURCE_TYPE is used to identify the type of resource you want to create. A resource type is identified by the name. The configuration parameters are essentially all the same.

In your example, you create a VPC network in AWS. The parameter you define is essentially the network mask you want to create.

First, to execute the plan, you need to download your provider. To do that, you need to execute the command terraform init. Open a command line, move to the folder where the file main.tf is saved, and execute the command terraform init:

```
Initializing the backend...

Initializing provider plugins...
- Checking for available provider plugins...
- Downloading plugin for provider "aws" (hashicorp/aws) 2.48.0...

The following providers do not have any version constraints in
configuration,
so the latest version was installed.

To prevent automatic upgrades to new major versions that may contain
breaking
```

changes, it is recommended to add version = "..." constraints to the
corresponding provider blocks in configuration, with the constraint strings
suggested below.

* provider.aws: version = "~> 2.48"

Terraform has been successfully initialized!

You may now begin working with Terraform. Try running terraform plan to
see any changes that are required for your infrastructure. All Terraform commands
should now work. If you ever set or change modules or the back-end configuration for
Terraform, rerun this command to reinitialize your working directory. If you forget, other
commands will detect it and remind you to do so if necessary.

Terraform is not configured, so the next step is to try to deploy the infrastructure, but
first you need to create the plan. To create the plan, open a command line and move to
the folder where the main.tf is saved and run the command terraform plan. The result
should be similar to this:

```
Refreshing Terraform state in-memory prior to plan...
The refreshed state will be used to calculate this plan, but will not be
persisted to local or remote state storage.
-------------------------------------------------------------------------

An execution plan has been generated and is shown below.
Resource actions are indicated with the following symbols:
  + create

Terraform will perform the following actions:

  # aws_vpc.hclbookvpc will be created
  + resource "aws_vpc" "hclbookvpc" {
      + arn                             = (known after apply)
      + assign_generated_ipv6_cidr_block = false
      + cidr_block                      = "20.0.0.0/16"
      + default_network_acl_id          = (known after apply)
      + default_route_table_id          = (known after apply)
      + default_security_group_id       = (known after apply)
      + dhcp_options_id                 = (known after apply)
```

```
    + enable_classiclink               = (known after apply)
    + enable_classiclink_dns_support   = (known after apply)
    + enable_dns_hostnames             = (known after apply)
    + enable_dns_support               = true
    + id                               = (known after apply)
    + instance_tenancy                 = "default"
    + ipv6_association_id              = (known after apply)
    + ipv6_cidr_block                  = (known after apply)
    + main_route_table_id              = (known after apply)
    + owner_id                         = (known after apply)
  }

Plan: 1 to add, 0 to change, 0 to destroy.

--------------------------------------------------------------------------
Note: You didn't specify an "-out" parameter to save this plan, so
Terraform can't guarantee that exactly these actions will be performed if
"terraform apply" is subsequently run.
```

The command `plan` shows the steps executed by Terraform to apply and create your infrastructure. You don't define most of the values; they are assigned after the creation of the resource. To apply the plan, you need to execute the command `apply`. In the same command line, run the command `terraform apply`.

An execution plan has been generated and is shown below. Resource actions are indicated with the following symbols:

```
  + create
```

Terraform will perform the following actions:

```
  # aws_vpc.hclbookvpc will be created
  + resource "aws_vpc" "hclbookvpc" {
      + arn                            = (known after apply)
      + assign_generated_ipv6_cidr_block = false
      + cidr_block                     = "20.0.0.0/16"
      + default_network_acl_id         = (known after apply)
      + default_route_table_id         = (known after apply)
      + default_security_group_id      = (known after apply)
```

```
    + dhcp_options_id                    = (known after apply)
    + enable_classiclink                 = (known after apply)
    + enable_classiclink_dns_support     = (known after apply)
    + enable_dns_hostnames               = (known after apply)
    + enable_dns_support                 = true
    + id                                 = (known after apply)
    + instance_tenancy                   = "default"
    + ipv6_association_id                = (known after apply)
    + ipv6_cidr_block                    = (known after apply)
    + main_route_table_id                = (known after apply)
    + owner_id                           = (known after apply)
  }

Plan: 1 to add, 0 to change, 0 to destroy.

Do you want to perform these actions?
  Terraform will perform the actions described above.
  Only 'yes' will be accepted to approve.

  Enter a value: yes

aws_vpc.hclbookvpc: Creating...
aws_vpc.hclbookvpc: Creation complete after 5s [id=vpc-02c8693c70b2d6d4c]
```

Insert the value "yes" when requested and you'll see Terraform create the VPC. To check the new VPC, connect to AWS and move to the VPC section. Figure 5-2 shows our VPC correctly created on the server.

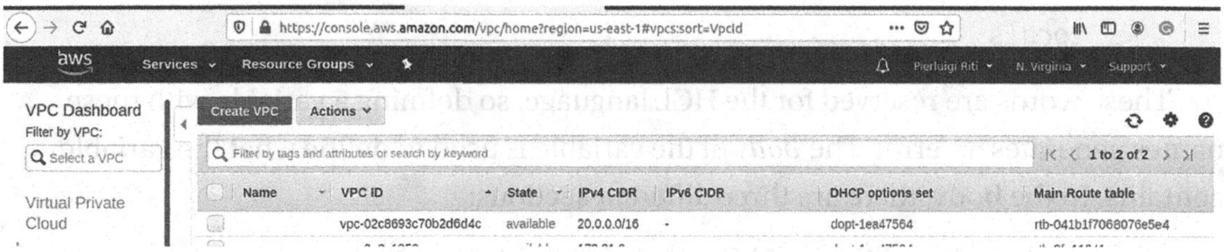

Figure 5-2. *The VPC instance created on AWS*

Variable HCL Terraform Configuration

The first example creates a simple Terraform configuration but in a real environment you probably need to create a variable configuration file because the same infrastructure can be deployed in a different environment. For example, it is possible to deploy in a development environment, stage environment, or production environment.

In HCL, it is possible to create a variable that is essentially a value you can send from the input to change the way the program executes the steps *input variables*. The variable in HCL has this syntax:

```
variable "NAME" {
    [BODY]
}
```

The *name* must start with a letter and must be followed by a letter, number, underscore (_), and hyphen (-). A variable can have any name except for some reserved words:

- source

- version

- providers

- count

- for_each

- lifecycle

- depends_on

- locals

These words are reserved for the HCL language, so defining a variable with these names generates an error. The *body* of the variable is used to define what the variable contains. In the body, there are three different sections:

- *Description:* This is used for descriptive purposes to document the variable. It is a good practice to document and describe the usage plus the scope of the variable

- *Type:* The type restricts the values that can be assigned to the variable. The type of variable in HCL can be string, number, or bool. It is possible to use the type constructor. This is used to create the complex type variable type. In HCL, it is possible to define two types of complex types. collections type, list(TYPE), map(TYPE), set(TYPE), all define a list of values of the same types. For instance, `list(string)` defines a list of strings. The structural type is used to group different types of variables. There are two types of structural types: object and tuple.

- *Default:* Default is the way to assign a default value to a variable. The default value is used if there is no value assigned to the variable.

Variables are normally configured in a file called `variable.tf`. This file is used to define the variable. In case of the default value, do not hard code the value. To better understand the concept of the variable, update your `main.tf` to have a variable mask address for the VPC. See Listing 5-7.

Listing 5-7. The New main.tf with the Variable Defined

```
provider "aws" {
  region = "us-east-1"
}

# Create a VPC
resource "aws_vpc" "hclbookvpc" {
  cidr_block = var.ip_range
}
```

The code now uses now *interpolation* to create the value for the `cidr_block`. The variable is defined in the file `variable.tf`. See Listing 5-8.

Listing 5-8. The variable.tf File for Creating the Variable Used in the main.tf

```
variable "ip_range" {
  description = "The IP Range we want to create for our VPC"
  type        = "string"
  default     = "20.0.0.0/16"
}
```

95

To pass the value of the variable in Terraform, you simply pass the value in the command line when you run the `plan` command:

```
terraform plan -var ip_range=10.1.0.0/16
```

When this command is executed, you can perceive the difference parameter sent to the plan; see Listing 5-9.

Listing 5-9. The Result of the Terraform Without Specifying the Variable

```
Refreshing Terraform state in-memory prior to plan...
The refreshed state will be used to calculate this plan, but will not be
persisted to local or remote state storage.

------------------------------------------------------------------------

An execution plan has been generated and is shown below.
Resource actions are indicated with the following symbols:
  + create

Terraform will perform the following actions:

  # aws_vpc.hclbookvpc will be created
  + resource "aws_vpc" "hclbookvpc" {
      + arn                            = (known after apply)
      + assign_generated_ipv6_cidr_block = false
      + cidr_block                     = "10.1.0.0/16"
      + default_network_acl_id         = (known after apply)
      + default_route_table_id         = (known after apply)
      + default_security_group_id      = (known after apply)
      + dhcp_options_id                = (known after apply)
      + enable_classiclink             = (known after apply)
      + enable_classiclink_dns_support = (known after apply)
      + enable_dns_hostnames           = (known after apply)
      + enable_dns_support             = true
      + id                             = (known after apply)
      + instance_tenancy               = "default"
      + ipv6_association_id            = (known after apply)
```

```
    + ipv6_cidr_block               = (known after apply)
    + main_route_table_id           = (known after apply)
    + owner_id                      = (known after apply)
  }
```

Plan: 1 to add, 0 to change, 0 to destroy.

Note: You didn't specify an "-out" parameter to save this plan, so
Terraform can't guarantee that exactly these actions will be performed if
"terraform apply" is subsequently run.

Now you can see that the cidr_block has the value 10.1.0.0/16, the same value you
assigned to the variable. You have created the file variable.tf. This is used in case
the variable is not sent via the command line. To see how HCL interacts, you can run
another plan command and see the result, which is shown in Listing 5-10.

Listing 5-10. The Result of Terraform with the Variable Specified

Refreshing Terraform state in-memory prior to plan...
The refreshed state will be used to calculate this plan, but will not be
persisted to local or remote state storage.

An execution plan has been generated and is shown below.
Resource actions are indicated with the following symbols:
  + create

Terraform will perform the following actions:

  # aws_vpc.hclbookvpc will be created
  + resource "aws_vpc" "hclbookvpc" {
      + arn   = (known after apply)
      + assign_generated_ipv6_cidr_block = false
      + cidr_block   = "20.0.0.0/16"
  ....

Note: You didn't specify an "-out" parameter to save this plan, so
Terraform can't guarantee that exactly these actions will be performed if
"terraform apply" is subsequently run.

This time you executed the command plan without the variable and you can see the
value for the cidr_block is the default value configured in the variable.tf.

The syntax shown in the example refers to Terraform version 0.12 and up.
The variable in the previous version of Terraform is indicated with the syntax
${<variable>}. For example, in the VPS code, you have a variable ${var.
ip_range}. In Terraform 0.12, you use this syntax: var.ip_range. This type of
syntax is called a *first-class expression* and is a new feature of the HCL syntax.

Because you want to use a specific version of Terraform (HCL2), you need to update
the main.tf and specify the minimum version of Terraform you want to use:

```
terraform{
      required_version => "0.12.0"
}
```

The new main.tf is shown in Listing 5-11.

Listing 5-11. The main.tf with the Terraform Version Specified

```
terraform {
  required_version = ">= 0.12"
}

provider "aws" {
  region = "us-east-1"
}

# Create a VPC
resource "aws_vpc" "hclbookvpc" {
  cidr_block = var.ip_range
}
```

This is just an introduction to the new HCL2 variable. In the next chapter, you will see how to create a `for` loop for reading elements in the map and list(s).

Looping with HCL

In HCL2, Hashicorp introduces a `for` loop. This is used for looping across the list and map created in HCL. Before HCL2, this was not feasible.

HCL2 creates a new operator to iterate the list and substitute with an element. An example of the operator is shown in Listing 5-12.

Listing 5-12. The New Loop in HCL

```
terraform {
  required_version = ">= 0.12"
}

provider "aws" {
  region = "us-east-1"
}

variable "vpc_id" {
  description = "ID for the AWS VPC where a security group is to be
  created."
}

variable "subnet_numbers" {
    description = "List of 8-bit numbers of subnets of base_cidr_block that
    should be granted access."
  default = [1, 2, 3]
}

data "aws_vpc" "hclbook" {
  id = var.vpc_id
}

resource "aws_security_group" "hclbook_example" {
  name       = "hclsubnet"
  vpc_id     = var.vpc_id
```

```
  ingress {
    from_port = 0
    to_port   = 0
    protocol  = -1

    cidr_blocks = [
      for num in var.subnet_numbers:
      cidrsubnet(data.aws_vpc.hclbook.cidr_block, 8, num)
    ]
  }
}
```

The code shows how to use the for loop in HCL. The code defines the subnet_
numbers which are the numbers of the subnet you want to create. The for loop is used in
the cidr_blocks:

```
cidr_blocks = [
  for num in var.subnet_numbers:
  cidrsubnet(data.aws_vpc.hclbook_example.cidr_block, 8, num)
]
```

This code creates a new cidr_blocks. For each value represented by the variable num
in subnet_numbers, it extends the CIDR prefix of the requested VPC to produce a subnet
CIDR prefix. For the default value of subnet_numbers above and a VPC CIDR prefix of
10.1.0.0/16, this would produce: ["10.1.1.0/24", "10.1.2.0/24", "10.1.3.0/24"].

To execute the code, you can use the same VPC you created previously. The ID for
the VPC is the input parameter for the new code. It is possible to get the information and
the VPC ID. Simply connect to your AWS account, move the VPC section, and get the
VPC ID from the account; see Figure 5-3. To run the code, it is just necessary to send the
VPC ID (in our case, vpc-0432ddccb9cafcccf) to the command line:

```
terraform apply -var vpc_id="vpc-0432ddccb9cafcccf"
```

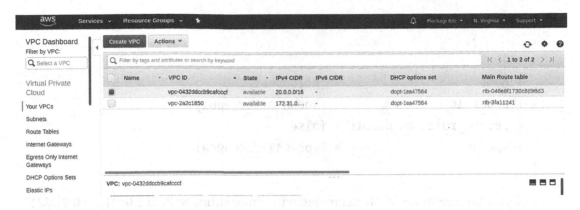

Figure 5-3. *The VPC screen on AWS*

Terraform applies the new HCL and resolves the for loop for the actual VPC. The results are shown in Listing 5-13.

Listing 5-13. The Result of the for Loop

```
# aws_security_group.hclbook_example will be created
+ resource "aws_security_group" "hclbook_example" {
    + arn                  = (known after apply)
    + description          = "Managed by Terraform"
    + egress               = (known after apply)
    + id                   = (known after apply)
    + ingress              = [
      + {
          + cidr_blocks      = [
            + "20.0.1.0/24",
            + "20.0.2.0/24",
            + "20.0.3.0/24",
          ]
          + description      = ""
          + from_port        = 0
          + ipv6_cidr_blocks = []
          + prefix_list_ids  = []
          + protocol         = "-1"
          + security_groups  = []
          + self             = false
```

```
              + to_port            = 0
          },
      ]
    + name                   = "hclsubnet"
    + owner_id               = (known after apply)
    + revoke_rules_on_delete = false
    + vpc_id                 = "vpc-0432ddccb9cafcccf"
  }
```

Now you can see the cidr_block created with three subnets: 20.0.1.0/24, 20.0.2.0/24 and 20.0.3.0/24. These values were created by the for loop. To change the subnet_numbers with the number we indicate, 1, 2, or 3. The for loop is very useful when, for example, you need to create subnets or you want to define the same image in more than one region or if you want to define more than one subnet for the network.

Advanced HCL/Terraform Parsing

HCL and Terraform are written using the Go language. With HCL, it is possible to create any type of configuration but if you want to have the maximum flexibility for your IaC, it is possible to extend your program using a GPL language such as Go. An example of a Go program used to generate an HCL is shown in Listing 5-14.

Listing 5-14. The Go Program Used to Generate an HCL File

```go
package main

import (
      "fmt"

      "github.com/hashicorp/hcl2/gohcl"
      "github.com/hashicorp/hcl2/hclwrite"
)

type Service struct {
      Name string   `hcl:"name,label"`
      Exe  []string `hcl:"executable"`
}
```

```go
type Constraints struct {
    OS    string `hcl:"os"`
    Arch string `hcl:"arch"`
}
type App struct {
    Name        string        `hcl:"name"`
    Desc        string        `hcl:"description"`
    Constraints *Constraints `hcl:"constraints,block"`
    Services    []Service     `hcl:"service,block"`
}
func main(){
    app := App{
        Name: "hclbookgo-app",
        Desc: "First application created with Golang",
        Constraints: &Constraints{
            OS:   "linux",
            Arch: "amd64",
        },
        Services: []Service{
            {
                Name: "web",
                Exe:  []string{"./web", "--listen=:8080"},
            },
            {
                Name: "worker",
                Exe:  []string{"./worker"},
            },
        },
    }

    f := hclwrite.NewEmptyFile()
    gohcl.EncodeIntoBody(&app, f.Body())
    fmt.Printf("%s", f.Bytes())
}
```

This program defines some structures used to define the *service* and the *constraints.* The code imports two important libraries used to create and manage the HCL file: github.com/hashicorp/hcl2/gohcl and github.com/hashicorp/hcl2/hclwrite. These two libraries are the parser libraries used to create the new HCL file.

The function to write the file is essentially these three lines:

```
f := hclwrite.NewEmptyFile()
gohcl.EncodeIntoBody(&app, f.Body())
fmt.Printf("%s", f.Bytes())
```

These three lines create a new file and attach the structure created as a body of the file.

To run the program, you need to first import the missing library. In Go, you can import the library from GitHub with a simple command-line command: go get. In your case, to import the library, you use go get github.com/hashicorp/hcl2/gohcl and go get github.com/hashicorp/hcl2/hclwrite. With these two libraries imported, you can run the program. See Listing 5-15.

Listing 5-15. The HCL Result of Running the Go Program

```
go run main.go
name        = "hclbookgo-app "
description = "First application created with Golang "

constraints {
  os   = "linux"
  arch = "amd64"
}

service "web" {
  executable = ["./web", "--listen=:8080"]
}
service "worker" {
  executable = ["./worker"]
}
```

Now you can see that the HCL file has the structure defined in your Go program. The HCL Parser is very useful when you want to create and define more complex HCL files.

Conclusion

This chapter shows the HCL used for Terraform: HCL2. HCL in general was born to work with Terraform. HCL is very useful for defining IaC. In this chapter, you started to use HCL to create more complex code with more complex configurations. Of course, you have just a basic idea about the HCL and you will learn more in the following chapters. You also saw how to use Go and the hclparser library to create your HCL. To use Go to create the HCL, you are allowed the opportunity to create a more powerful and complex HCL. Go can bypass the natural limitations of the HCL language and it is therefore possible to create a complete program with of course more complex logic. In the following chapters, you will learn more about HCL and how to use Go to create the HCL and save it in a file. To have a HCL fully defined in a file and created by a GPL language like Go facilitates a complete SDLC and makes your IaC fully compliant with best engineering practices.

CHAPTER 6

Consul HCL

With the birth of a new architecture pattern, like the microservice architecture, the necessity of a service registry with discovery became evident. Consul offers a solution for managing and maintaining service discovery. In this chapter, you will learn how to use Consul and how to configure it using the HCL language.

Introduction to Consul

Consul is a service network solution used to connect and secure services across different platforms including both private and public clouds.

Consul fits different use cases, which makes the product ideal for most of the actual microservices or mesh service architectures. Some of the use cases are as follows:

- *Service register/discovery*: Consul uses the client to learn about the service. The service can be queried using a DNS or HTTP API. This is probably the main use case for Consul.

- *Health check*: The Consul client can be used to perform some basic health checks on the server. For example, it is possible to check memory usage or to ascertain if the necessary services are indeed reachable.

- *Key/value store*: Consul has a key/value feature. This feature can be used in a lot of different scenarios such as a dynamic configuration. The feature is exposed via an HTTP API.

- *Securing the service communication*: With Consul it is possible to generate a TLS certificate to enable communication across two different services. The certificate can be changed in real time to suit the most complex network configuration.

© Pierluigi Riti and David Flynn 2021
P. Riti and D. Flynn, *Beginning HCL Programming*, https://doi.org/10.1007/978-1-4842-6634-2_6

- *Support for multiple datacenters*: Consul can support the multiple data centers, which facilitates a reusable configuration in such scenarios.

These features make Consul useful for DevOps and developers facilitating an actual elastic, complex infrastructure.

Consul Architecture

Consul is a distributed and highly available system. The main utilization of Consul is to allow service discovery. This becomes important when the infrastructure is migrated from a traditional format to Infrastructure as Code. The Consul key/value feature and the service discovery feature help to better define and manage the service in the overall design infrastructure.

The Consul main component is the *Consul agent*. This is the core component. The agent is responsible for all operations. It maintains and creates the membership information on the cluster. The agent has to run in all nodes of the cluster. The agent can run in two modes:

- Server

- Client

The server node has more responsibility than a simple client. The server participates in the quorum necessary for the election of the leader.

When we talk about a Consul cluster, we mean a configuration with some agent running as a server and an n-number of the agents running as clients. In a Consul cluster, essentially we run one or more nodes as a server, and we connect one or more nodes as clients. A basic Consul architecture is shown in Figure 6-1.

When we create a Consul cluster, it is necessary to have a minimum of three to five servers. It is important to have the correct data replication. Later in this chapter, you will learn about the consensus protocol in its execution for the leader election.

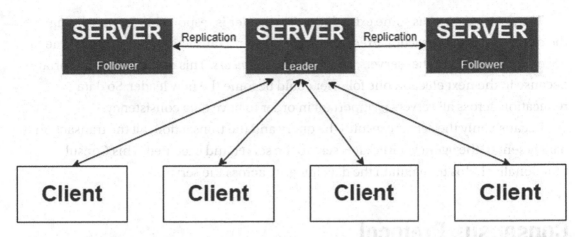

Figure 6-1. *A basic Consul architecture*

The leader is responsible for replicating the data collected from the client to the other servers. This is an important step to implement the correct functionality of the cluster. If the replication is broken, the cluster loses data replication, which can result in inconsistencies across the cluster.

All agents that participate in the cluster use the *gossip protocol*. The gossip protocol is used to create a gossip pool for all of the agents. This is not an implied distinction between agent and/or client. This pool is used for several purposes:

1. The client does not need to be configured. The discovery of the server is done automatically.

2. The failure detection for a node is done in a distributed manner. This is done by the internal distribution protocol used in Consul, where every node has self-awareness about its status. Because every node of the cluster self-checks its health, Consul has a more reliable failure detection.

3. The servers of the data center are all part of the Raft pool. Raft is a consensus algorithm. A consensus algorithm is a specific family of algorithms used to define a common value across a decentralized distributed system. Raft is used with the gossip protocol to define the leader of the Consul cluster.

The *server leader* has some extra duties. The leader is responsible for processing the query and the transaction executed on the cluster. Transactions at the same time are replicated to the other servers, known as the *followers*. This replication is important because in the next election one follower could become the new leader. So data replication across all servers is important in order to have data consistency.

Because only the server executes the query and the transaction, all the transaction data is sent to the agent via RPC. It is sent to the server and executed. This Consul functionality helps to maintain the data integrity across the server.

Consensus Protocol

The consensus protocol is a family of protocols used to solve a fundamental problem in information technology, particular in relation to *distributed computing*. The problem to be solved by the consensus protocol is to find a mechanism to guarantee an agreement over a result.

A consensus protocol requires an agreement across different agents. This agent may be unreachable or broken and for this reason the protocol must to be *fault tollerance* or *resilient*. The challenge of multi-agent computation has become famous because of Bitcoin. In reality, this protocol or approach is much older and was used across different areas for years. One real application of a consensus protocol is PageRank, developed by Google.

Consul use a consensus protocol called Raft, which is based on the Paxos consensus protocol. The main difference between Raft and Paxos is the fewer states and simpler algorithm which makes Raft easier to read and understand. The Raft protocol has three states:

1. The *follower* state

2. The *candidate* state

3. The *leader* state

In the Raft protocol, all the nodes start in the *follower* state. If a node does not hear from the leader, the follower node moves to the *candidate* state.

When a node becomes a *candidate*, it poses a vote to the other server nodes in the cluster. The nodes reply with their votes and the node that receives the most votes becomes the new *leader*. This process is called *leader election* and is used to define the leader in the Consul cluster. When the leader is elected, all data changes are send to the leader. The leader then propagates the changes to the followers. The followers commit the changes in their log entry and reply back to the leader to communicate that they have saved the values. When all of nodes have replicated to the leader, the leader writes the data in the log and communicates to the followers that the data is committed. At this stage, the cluster reaches a consensus on the value. This state is called *log replication*.

To analyse the Raft protocol, we need to introduce and explain some terms:

1. *Log*: Log is the basic unit for the Raft protocol. It solves the consistency challenge whereby Consul replicates the log across all server agents. This is essentially the log replication. In Consul, a log entry includes everything: new key-value pairs, adding new nodes, remove nodes, etc. The log remains valid until all of the nodes agree on the order of the entry in the log itself.

2. *Finite state machine*: A finite state machine, or FSM, is a mathematical model of computation. It is a collection of *finite states*. In Consul, when a new log is sent out by the server, the state machine moves the application from one state to another. The result of the state machine must be deterministic. This means the application of the same log entry on another node; the result of the state machine must be the same.

3. *Peer set*: The peer set is essentially all of the nodes that participate in the log replication. In Consul, a peer set is all of the server agents.

4. *Quorum*: Quorum refers to the minimum number of nodes necessary to reach an agreement. The quorum is calculated with this formula: *(n/2)+1*. For example, with a three-server node cluster, the quorum is (3/2)+1 = 2.5, so in this case 2.

With these definitions clarified, let's continue to analyze the Raft consensus protocol.

The scope of the book is not to explain the Raft protocol. To better understand the Raft protocol, refer to the original document at `https://raft.github.io/raft.pdf`.

In the Raft protocol implemented in Consul, all nodes can have one of three states: leader, follower, or candidate. The leader is responsible for sending the log entry to the other nodes. If a follower does not receive any message from the leader for a certain amount of time, the node reaches the *election timeout.* The election timeout is a random number between 150 ms and 300 ms. When a node reaches the timeout, the node changes state from follower to candidate. In the candidate state, the node votes for itself and then asks for a vote from the other nodes. If the other nodes don't vote for themselves, the nodes send in their vote to the candidate node. If the node reaches a quorum, it becomes the new leader. After expressing their vote, every node resets its election timeout.

When the new leader is elected, the leader starts sending *appended entries* to the follower nodes. These specific messages are sent to follow the time specified in the heartbeat timeout. The follower responds to the appended entries. This is used to check the status of the server nodes. When a follower stops receiving the appended entry message, the follower changes state from follower to candidate and a new election starts.

When the cluster has a new leader, every entry is received by the leader. When the cluster receives a new request, it sends out the appended entries to the follower. The follower replies to the message sent out by the leader. The response indicates that the log is successfully entered in the agent log. The leader writes the same entry in its log. When this action is performed, the entry is considered *committed*, and it can then be applied to the final state machine. In Consul, the finite state machine is application-specific and is built using MemDB. It is used to maintain the cluster state.

In Consul, the consensus protocol is used to reach *consistency*, as per the definition in the CAP theorem. The CAP theorem is a theoretical computer science theorem. In this theorem, the computer scientist Eric Brewer states that a distributed system can only have two out of its three essential properties working simultaneously. These properties are

1. *Consistency*: The ability to always return the most recent write for a given client

2. *Availability*: The ability of a non-failing node to always return a response in a reasonable time

3. *Partition tolerance*: The ability for the system to continue to work when one or more nodes have a failure

The consensus protocol is used in Consul to guarantee consistency across the nodes.

Installing Consul

The best way to learn how to use a software program is to get your hands dirty. You just learned the basic Consul architecture. This is important to understand. But of course, to use the software, you need to install it. To install Consul, the first step is to download the software itself. It can be downloaded from this address: `www.consul.io/downloads.html`. From the page, select the correct package and download it; see Figure 6-2.

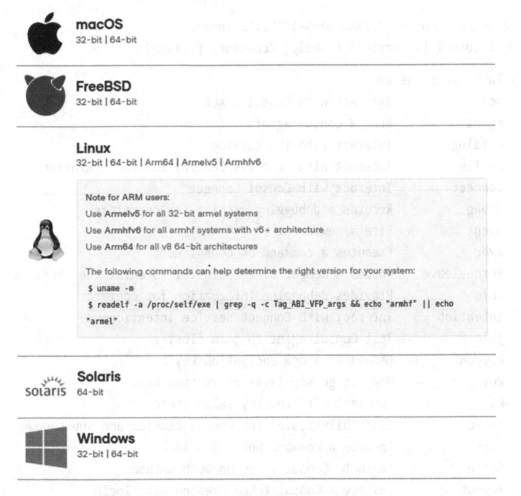

Figure 6-2. *The Consul page for downloading the software*

CHAPTER 6   CONSUL HCL

With the package downloaded, unpack the zip package and configure the path to point to the Consul executable. With the path updated, execute the following command:

consul

This command returns all of the commands you can use and execute with the actual agent. See Listing 6-1.

Listing 6-1. The Results of the consul Command

```
piggi@piggi-Lenovo-ideapad-320S-15AST:~$ consul
Usage: consul [--version] [--help] <command> [<args>]

Available commands are:
    acl          Interact with Consul's ACLs
    agent        Runs a Consul agent
    catalog      Interact with the catalog
    config       Interact with Consul's Centralized Configurations
    connect      Interact with Consul Connect
    debug        Records a debugging archive for operators
    event        Fire a new event
    exec         Executes a command on Consul nodes
    force-leave  Forces a member of the cluster to enter the "left" state
    info         Provides debugging information for operators.
    intention    Interact with Connect service intentions
    join         Tell Consul agent to join cluster
    keygen       Generates a new encryption key
    keyring      Manages gossip layer encryption keys
    kv           Interact with the key-value store
    leave        Gracefully leaves the Consul cluster and shuts down
    lock         Execute a command holding a lock
    login        Login to Consul using an auth method
    logout       Destroy a Consul token created with login
    maint        Controls node or service maintenance mode
    members      Lists the members of a Consul cluster
    monitor      Stream logs from a Consul agent
    operator     Provides cluster-level tools for Consul operators
    reload       Triggers the agent to reload configuration files
```

rtt	Estimates network round trip time between nodes
services	Interact with services
snapshot	Saves, restores and inspects snapshots of Consul server state
tls	Builtin helpers for creating CAs and certificates
validate	Validate config files/directories
version	Prints the Consul version
watch	Watch for changes in Consul

With Consul now configured, you can run the agent. You run it in your local environment, which will give you just one node. You can build a cluster later. Because you are in your local environment, you can create a developer node for use and start to test how Consul works.

Using Consul in developer mode is not scalable or secure. This means there is no replication and the data is not secure. This specific configuration should be used only for development.

In order to run a Consul agent in developer mode, you must use the argument -dev:

```
consul agent -dev
```

The output is usually as follows:

```
$ consul agent -dev
==> Starting Consul agent...
           Version: 'v1.7.2'
           Node ID: 'b40e7f07-6f9b-d87c-9431-a47c604d9857'
         Node name: 'piggi-Lenovo-ideapad-320S-15AST'
        Datacenter: 'dc1' (Segment: '<all>')
            Server: true (Bootstrap: false)
       Client Addr: [127.0.0.1] (HTTP: 8500, HTTPS: -1, gRPC: 8502, DNS: 8600)
      Cluster Addr: 127.0.0.1 (LAN: 8301, WAN: 8302)
           Encrypt: Gossip: false, TLS-Outgoing: false, TLS-Incoming:
           false, Auto-Encrypt-TLS: false
```

==> Log data will now stream in as it occurs:

```
2020-04-28T22:29:43.068+0100 [DEBUG] agent: Using random ID as node ID:
id=b40e7f07-6f9b-d87c-9431-a47c604d9857
2020-04-28T22:29:43.101+0100 [DEBUG] agent.tlsutil: Update: version=1
2020-04-28T22:29:43.105+0100 [DEBUG] agent.tlsutil: OutgoingRPCWrapper:
version=1
2020-04-28T22:29:43.154+0100 [INFO]  agent.server.raft: initial
configuration: index=1 servers="[{Suffrage:Voter ID:b40e7f07-6f9b-d87c-
9431-a47c604d9857 Address:127.0.0.1:8300}]"
2020-04-28T22:29:43.156+0100 [INFO]  agent.server.raft: entering
follower state: follower="Node at 127.0.0.1:8300 [Follower]" leader=
2020-04-28T22:29:43.157+0100 [INFO]  agent.server.serf.wan: serf:
EventMemberJoin: piggi-Lenovo-ideapad-320S-15AST.dc1 127.0.0.1
2020-04-28T22:29:43.158+0100 [INFO]  agent.server.serf.lan: serf:
EventMemberJoin: piggi-Lenovo-ideapad-320S-15AST 127.0.0.1
2020-04-28T22:29:43.163+0100 [INFO]  agent.server: Adding LAN server:
server="piggi-Lenovo-ideapad-320S-15AST (Addr: tcp/127.0.0.1:8300) (DC: dc1)"
2020-04-28T22:29:43.166+0100 [INFO]  agent: Started DNS server:
address=127.0.0.1:8600 network=udp
2020-04-28T22:29:43.166+0100 [INFO]  agent.server: Handled event for
server in area: event=member-join server=piggi-Lenovo-ideapad-320S-
15AST.dc1 area=wan
2020-04-28T22:29:43.166+0100 [INFO]  agent: Started DNS server:
address=127.0.0.1:8600 network=tcp
2020-04-28T22:29:43.168+0100 [INFO]  agent: Started HTTP server:
address=127.0.0.1:8500 network=tcp
2020-04-28T22:29:43.168+0100 [INFO]  agent: Started gRPC server:
address=127.0.0.1:8502 network=tcp
2020-04-28T22:29:43.170+0100 [INFO]  agent: started state syncer
```
==> Consul agent running!
```
2020-04-28T22:29:43.220+0100 [WARN]  agent.server.raft: heartbeat
timeout reached, starting election: last-leader=
2020-04-28T22:29:43.220+0100 [INFO]  agent.server.raft: entering
candidate state: node="Node at 127.0.0.1:8300 [Candidate]" term=2
```

2020-04-28T22:29:43.220+0100 [DEBUG] agent.server.raft: votes: needed=1
2020-04-28T22:29:43.220+0100 [DEBUG] agent.server.raft: vote granted:
from=b40e7f07-6f9b-d87c-9431-a47c604d9857 term=2 tally=1
2020-04-28T22:29:43.220+0100 [INFO] agent.server.raft: election won:
tally=1
2020-04-28T22:29:43.220+0100 [INFO] agent.server.raft: entering leader
state: leader="Node at 127.0.0.1:8300 [Leader]"
2020-04-28T22:29:43.220+0100 [INFO] agent.server: cluster leadership
acquired
Processing server acl mode for: piggi-Lenovo-ideapad-320S-15AST - 0
2020-04-28T22:29:43.220+0100 [INFO] agent.server: Cannot upgrade to
new ACLs: leaderMode=0 mode=0 found=true leader=127.0.0.1:8300
2020-04-28T22:29:43.221+0100 [INFO] agent.server: New leader elected:
payload=piggi-Lenovo-ideapad-320S-15AST
2020-04-28T22:29:43.393+0100 [DEBUG] connect.ca.consul: consul CA
provider configured: id=07:80:c8:de:f6:41:86:29:8f:9c:b8:17:d6:48:c2:d5
:c5:5c:7f:0c:03:f7:cf:97:5a:a7:c1:68:aa:23:ae:81 is_primary=true
2020-04-28T22:29:43.407+0100 [INFO] agent.server.connect: initialized
primary datacenter CA with provider: provider=consul
2020-04-28T22:29:43.407+0100 [INFO] agent.leader: started routine:
routine="CA root pruning"
2020-04-28T22:29:43.407+0100 [DEBUG] agent.server: Skipping self join
check for node since the cluster is too small: node=piggi-Lenovo-
ideapad-320S-15AST
2020-04-28T22:29:43.407+0100 [INFO] agent.server: member joined,
marking health alive: member=piggi-Lenovo-ideapad-320S-15AST
2020-04-28T22:29:43.595+0100 [DEBUG] agent: Skipping remote check since
it is managed automatically: check=serfHealth
2020-04-28T22:29:43.595+0100 [INFO] agent: Synced node info
2020-04-28T22:29:44.737+0100 [DEBUG] agent: Skipping remote check since
it is managed automatically: check=serfHealth
2020-04-28T22:29:44.738+0100 [DEBUG] agent: Node info in sync
2020-04-28T22:29:44.738+0100 [DEBUG] agent: Node info in sync
2020-04-28T22:29:45.393+0100 [DEBUG] agent.tlsutil: OutgoingRPCWrapper:
version=1

The log shows all of the steps of the Raft protocol. The first state is the heartbeat timeout (1). The node then changes state to the candidate (2) state. The log shows the election and the number of votes the node needs to be elected (3). The next step is the result of the election (4). The cluster now is active and has a specific leader for the operations. If you want to see how the cluster is made at the moment, you can use the argument `members`.

To see the actual status of the cluster, open a new command-line window, and use the command for checking members:

```
consul members
```

The result of the command is the status of the cluster with all of the members:

Node	Address	Status	Type	Build	Protocol	DC	Segment
piggi-Lenovo-							
ideapad-320S-15AST	127.0.0.1:8301	alive	server	1.7.2	2	dc1	<all>

The result shows the IP of the agent, the auto-generated name, and some details such as status and type.

It is possible to have more detailed information about the cluster members by using the argument `detailed`. The command line code is `consul members - detailed`.

The `members` command is executed against the client. The client gets the information using the gossip protocol. This protocol is used to broadcast the data across the different nodes of the cluster. The protocol utilizes the Serf library, which is a specific library created by HashiCorp. The gossip protocol moves the data across the data centers. In this scenario, it can only be local, which mean a LAN gossip pool. For a remote data center, it is a WAN gossip pool. Using the Serf library, Consul can manage entire failures across the data center. This can be a single node failure or an entire WAN pool failure.

In addition to the `members` command, it is possible to have information about the node of the agent using the HTTP API. This API is used to maintain most of the Consul operations and is a great way to interact with Consul itself. You can interrogate the HTTP API with this command:

```
curl localhost:8500/v1/catalog/nodes
```

The result shows the JSON response with all of the nodes:

```
[
    {
        "ID": "07969187-2970-5420-dc4d-f5d8833430b6",
        "Node": "piggi-Lenovo-ideapad-320S-15AST",
        "Address": "127.0.0.1",
        "Datacenter": "dc1",
        "TaggedAddresses": {
            "lan": "127.0.0.1",
            "lan_ipv4": "127.0.0.1",
            "wan": "127.0.0.1",
            "wan_ipv4": "127.0.0.1"
        },
        "Meta": {
            "consul-network-segment": ""
        },
        "CreateIndex": 10,
        "ModifyIndex": 11
    }
]
```

In Consul, there is another way to discover the nodes of the pool using the DNS interface.

The Consul DNS interface allows connections with Consul without excessive interaction or deep integration. The primary use of the DNS interface is to allow service discovery. To use the DNS interface, use the tool dig. For example, you can try in your machine with this command:

```
dig @127.0.0.1 -p 8600 <your node name>
```

The command will return the information about the server with the name specified:

```
~$ dig @127.0.0.1 -p 8600 piggi-Lenovo-ideapad-320S-15AST (1)
```

```
; <<>> DiG 9.11.5-P4-5.1ubuntu2.1-Ubuntu <<>> @127.0.0.1 -p 8600 piggi-
Lenovo-ideapad-320S-15AST
; (1 server found)
;; global options: +cmd
;; Got answer:
;; ->>HEADER<<- opcode: QUERY, status: SERVFAIL, id: 16841
;; flags: qr rd; QUERY: 1, ANSWER: 0, AUTHORITY: 0, ADDITIONAL: 0
;; WARNING: recursion requested but not available

;; QUESTION SECTION:
;piggi-Lenovo-ideapad-320S-15AST.  IN     A

;; Query time: 0 msec
;; SERVER: 127.0.0.1#8600(127.0.0.1)
;; WHEN: Tue Apr 28 22:36:46 IST 2020
;; MSG SIZE  rcvd: 49
```

Above you can see the call in which we sent the node name. Consul replied with some basic information. The last step for the first exploration of Consul is to learn how to gracefully stop the agent. To stop the agent, use the command leave:

```
consul leave
```

The result is simple:

```
Graceful leave complete
```

You now understand how to spin up and down a simple Consul agent. Now you'll learn how to start it in development mode; this can be used to breed confidence with the Consul service itself.

Defining the Service in Consul

The primary goal of Consul is service discovery. The agent is responsible for locating the service discovery. To locate the service, every agent needs to be configured with the basic information about which service you want to locate and check.

To register a service, Consul offers the command services plus the subcommands register and deregister. For example, you can use this syntax to register a new service to monitor:

```
consul services register -name=iis
```

This creates a configuration file named iis. The result is a JSON configuration file similar to the one shown in Listing 6-2.

Listing 6-2. The Consul File iis.json

```
{
  "Service": {
    "Name": "iis"
  }
}
```

The JSON created can be now be used to register the service with the command register:

```
consul services register iis.json
```

This command registers the service in Consul and tells the agent to start monitoring the health check of the service itself:

```
~/hcl_vault_code$ consul services register iis.json
Registered service: iis
```

If you take a look on the Consul debug window, you will see something similar to this:

```
2020-04-28T22:40:36.565+0100 [INFO]  agent: Synced service: service=iis
2020-04-28T22:40:36.565+0100 [DEBUG] agent.http: Request finished:
method=PUT url=/v1/agent/service/register from=127.0.0.1:51442
latency=22.179091ms
2020-04-28T22:40:36.565+0100 [DEBUG] agent: Node info in sync
2020-04-28T22:40:36.565+0100 [DEBUG] agent: Service in sync:
service=iis
2020-04-28T22:40:36.565+0100 [DEBUG] agent: Node info in sync
```

```
2020-04-28T22:40:36.565+0100 [DEBUG] agent: Service in sync:
service=iis
2020-04-28T22:40:40.069+0100 [DEBUG] agent: Skipping remote check since
it is managed automatically: check=serfHealth
2020-04-28T22:40:40.069+0100 [DEBUG] agent: Node info in sync
2020-04-28T22:40:40.069+0100 [DEBUG] agent: Service in sync:
service=iis
```

Consul starts to register the service. The next step to execute is to sync the node to make the service available on all of the nodes. To deregister the service, it is possible to use the command `deregister` or `-id`:

```
consul services deregister iis.json
```

or

```
consul services -id iss.json
```

The result of the command shows the service completely deregistered from the agent:

```
~/hcl_vault_code$ consul services deregister iis.json
Deregistered service: iis
```

The most common way to define the service is to create a *service definition*. This is a file used to create and define the service. The service definition can be in a directory where you can have more than one file.

To create a service definition, you use the HCL language or the JSON file. The aim of this book is teach you about the HCL so we'll show how to use the HCL to create the service definition.

HCL for Service Definition

The first step when creating a service is to define the folder where this service will be configured. In the Linux environment, this is a folder with the extension .d. Let's create the service with this syntax:

```
mkdir ./consul.d
```

This command is used to create a folder called consul.d. Initially you create a new service similar to IIS using the JSON to define the service; see Listing 6-3.

Listing 6-3. The New Consul Service Defined in the consul.d Folder

```
{ "service":
  { "name": "web",
    "tags": ["rails"],
    "port": 80
  }
}
```

Save the file with the name of web.json. To run the script, Consul requires you to specify the location of the config dir. It is possible to do this using the parameter config-dir. Another important parameter is enable-local-script-checks, as in this service:

```
{"name": "web",
 "tags": ["rails"],
 "port": 80
}
```

The } parameter is used to evaluate the script and identify any issues or vulnerabilities in the script. To complete the call of the script, enter

```
consul agent -dev -enable-script-checks -config-dir=./consul.d
```

The result of the command shows the agent running with the specified configuration. See Listing 6-4.

Listing 6-4. The Consul Result for the Check Service

```
==> Starting Consul agent...
         Version: 'v1.7.2'
         Node ID: 'a2629b6a-3225-bc63-2205-7da36593ebc3'
       Node name: 'piggi-Lenovo-ideapad-320S-15AST'
      Datacenter: 'dc1' (Segment: '<all>')
          Server: true (Bootstrap: false)
     Client Addr: [127.0.0.1] (HTTP: 8500, HTTPS: -1, gRPC: 8502, DNS: 8600)
    Cluster Addr: 127.0.0.1 (LAN: 8301, WAN: 8302)
```

       Encrypt: Gossip: false, TLS-Outgoing: false, TLS-Incoming:
       false, Auto-Encrypt-TLS: false

==> Log data will now stream in as it occurs:

2020-04-19T17:54:10.712+0100 [DEBUG] agent: Using random ID as node ID:
id=a2629b6a-3225-bc63-2205-7da36593ebc3
2020-04-19T17:54:10.715+0100 [DEBUG] agent.tlsutil: Update: version=1
2020-04-19T17:54:10.739+0100 [DEBUG] agent.tlsutil: OutgoingRPCWrapper:
version=1
2020-04-19T17:54:10.968+0100 [INFO] agent.server.raft: initial
configuration: index=1 servers="[{Suffrage:Voter ID:a2629b6a-3225-bc63-
2205-7da36593ebc3 Address:127.0.0.1:8300}]"
2020-04-19T17:54:10.971+0100 [INFO] agent.server.raft: entering
follower state: follower="Node at 127.0.0.1:8300 [Follower]" leader=
2020-04-19T17:54:11.005+0100 [INFO] agent.server.serf.wan: serf:
EventMemberJoin: piggi-Lenovo-ideapad-320S-15AST.dc1 127.0.0.1
2020-04-19T17:54:11.006+0100 [INFO] agent.server.serf.lan: serf:
EventMemberJoin: piggi-Lenovo-ideapad-320S-15AST 127.0.0.1
2020-04-19T17:54:11.012+0100 [INFO] agent.server: Adding LAN server:
server="piggi-Lenovo-ideapad-320S-15AST (Addr: tcp/127.0.0.1:8300)
(DC: dc1)"
2020-04-19T17:54:11.012+0100 [INFO] agent.server: Handled event for
server in area: event=member-join server=piggi-Lenovo-ideapad-320S-
15AST.dc1 area=wan
2020-04-19T17:54:11.098+0100 [INFO] agent: Started DNS server:
address=127.0.0.1:8600 network=tcp
2020-04-19T17:54:11.098+0100 [WARN] agent.server.raft: heartbeat
timeout reached, starting election: last-leader=
2020-04-19T17:54:11.098+0100 [INFO] agent.server.raft: entering
candidate state: node="Node at 127.0.0.1:8300 [Candidate]" term=2
2020-04-19T17:54:11.098+0100 [DEBUG] agent.server.raft: votes: needed=1
2020-04-19T17:54:11.098+0100 [DEBUG] agent.server.raft: vote granted:
from=a2629b6a-3225-bc63-2205-7da36593ebc3 term=2 tally=1
2020-04-19T17:54:11.098+0100 [INFO] agent.server.raft: election won:
tally=1

```
2020-04-19T17:54:11.098+0100 [INFO]  agent.server.raft: entering leader
state: leader="Node at 127.0.0.1:8300 [Leader]"
2020-04-19T17:54:11.099+0100 [INFO]  agent.server: cluster leadership
acquired
 Processing server acl mode for: piggi-Lenovo-ideapad-320S-15AST - 0
2020-04-19T17:54:11.099+0100 [INFO]  agent.server: Cannot upgrade to
new ACLs: leaderMode=0 mode=0 found=true leader=127.0.0.1:8300
2020-04-19T17:54:11.101+0100 [DEBUG] connect.ca.consul: consul CA
provider configured: id=07:80:c8:de:f6:41:86:29:8f:9c:b8:17:d6:48:c2:d5
:c5:5c:7f:0c:03:f7:cf:97:5a:a7:c1:68:aa:23:ae:81 is_primary=true
2020-04-19T17:54:11.111+0100 [INFO]  agent.server: New leader elected:
payload=piggi-Lenovo-ideapad-320S-15AST
2020-04-19T17:54:11.117+0100 [INFO]  agent.server.connect: initialized
primary datacenter CA with provider: provider=consul
2020-04-19T17:54:11.117+0100 [INFO]  agent.leader: started routine:
routine="CA root pruning"
2020-04-19T17:54:11.117+0100 [DEBUG] agent.server: Skipping self join
check for node since the cluster is too small: node=piggi-Lenovo-
ideapad-320S-15AST
2020-04-19T17:54:11.117+0100 [INFO]  agent.server: member joined,
marking health alive: member=piggi-Lenovo-ideapad-320S-15AST
2020-04-19T17:54:11.250+0100 [INFO]   agent: Started DNS server:
address=127.0.0.1:8600 network=udp
2020-04-19T17:54:11.251+0100 [INFO]   agent: Started HTTP server:
address=127.0.0.1:8500 network=tcp
2020-04-19T17:54:11.252+0100 [INFO]   agent: Started gRPC server:
address=127.0.0.1:8502 network=tcp
2020-04-19T17:54:11.252+0100 [INFO]   agent: started state syncer
==> Consul agent running!
2020-04-19T17:54:11.478+0100 [DEBUG] agent: Skipping remote check since
it is managed automatically: check=serfHealth
2020-04-19T17:54:11.479+0100 [INFO]   agent: Synced node info
2020-04-19T17:54:11.479+0100 [INFO]   agent: Synced service: service=web
2020-04-19T17:54:11.479+0100 [DEBUG] agent: Node info in sync
```

```
2020-04-19T17:54:11.479+0100 [DEBUG] agent: Service in sync:
service=web
2020-04-19T17:54:11.744+0100 [DEBUG] agent: Skipping remote check since
it is managed automatically: check=serfHealth
2020-04-19T17:54:11.744+0100 [DEBUG] agent: Node info in sync
2020-04-19T17:54:11.744+0100 [DEBUG] agent: Service in sync:
service=web
2020-04-19T17:54:13.112+0100 [DEBUG] agent.tlsutil: OutgoingRPCWrapper:
version=1
```

Using JSON is useful but it's not the scope of the book. Now you use HCL to configure a service. The code is shown in Listing 6-5.

Listing 6-5. The HCL Code to Check a Redis Service

```
services {
  id = "redis0" (1)
  name = "redis" (2)
  tags = [ (3)
    "primary"
  ]
  address = ""
  port = 6000
  checks = [ (4)
    {
      args = ["/bin/check_redis", "-p", "6000"]
      interval = "10s"
      timeout = "30s"
    }
  ]
}
```

The HCL code is used to check and configure the Redis service in the system and to perform a health check of the service.

The first two lines, (1) and (2), are used to define the name of the service and the id for the service itself. Every service needs a `name`, which is mandatory for the Consul definition; `id` and `tags` are optional values for the Consul service. In the code, the `tags` are defined in line (3). Line (4) is where the service is configured for the health check. This section defines the type of check that needs to be executed for the service.

Conclusion

This chapter introduced Consul. This software is useful when you want to create a layer for service discovery or service mesh. Consul has a lot of use cases, which are not the scope of this book. The purpose is to introduce and explain Consul. We showed some basic configuration for Consul. In later chapters, you will use Consul to create a full IaC.

CHAPTER 7

Vault HCL

Vault is the software component from the HashiCorp family used to manage secrets. Everyday work involves a lot of *secrets* such as passwords, private keys used to connect to different servers, etc. HashiCorp Vault is easy to use to manage all of these secrets. Vault can be easily integrated with external software or with a different cloud vendor. In this chapter, you will learn how to use and configure Vault for daily use.

Introduction to Vault

Vault is a tool for securely managing secrets. The term *secrets* is intended to cover anything we want to protect such as passwords, API keys, certificates, and everything we think needs protection.

Vault provides a unified interface for the management and creation of secrets in our system. Vault creates a very detailed audit log. This is very important for every company as the audit log is key to demonstrating the "due care and due diligence" necessary for maintaining a good level of cyber security.

A modern system architecture is normally a mix of different layers and sometimes a hybrid-type cloud setup. All of these technologies and different layers need to share secrets like API keys to be used in the code or private keys for access to network segments. For all of these secrets, Vault can be the perfect solution.

© Pierluigi Riti and David Flynn 2021
P. Riti and D. Flynn, *Beginning HCL Programming*, https://doi.org/10.1007/978-1-4842-6634-2_7

Vault can be easily programmed and expanded. This is manifested in the system when we want to know who has had access plus where and when, or if we need to update the audit log. This is the very power of Vault. Vault can be easily programmed through its dynamic API interface. This API can be easily used to develop and integrate the Vault engine in our program and infrastructure. Vault can fill different use cases:

1. *Secure and store secrets*: It is possible to store different types of secrets from user passwords to API keys. The storage can be, for example, a disk or a Consul cluster. All secrets are encrypted, which enhances security.

2. *Dynamic secrets*: This is one of the most interesting features of Vault. It is possible to create a secret to be used, for example, in AWS. When the secret is requested, Vault creates the secret with a valid username/secret, allowing the operation and then destroying the secret.

3. *Data encryption*: It is possible to encrypt/decrypt data without the necessity of storing it in Vault. This can be used, for example, to encrypt the data first to save it in another location like a SQL server or a file system. The data can be decrypted using Vault.

4. *Secret leasing and renewal*: When a new secret is created in Vault, it has a *lease*, which means every secret has a specific time frame. At the end of the lease, the secret is destroyed and automatically renewed with a new automatically generated password.

5. *Secret revocation*: Vault was built with the management of secrets in mind. This means one of the usages is to revoke a secret. This functionality can be used for certificate renewal as well as to lock a system in case of any intrusion.

All these use cases make Vault the perfect choice for secret management. In addition, Vault can be easily integrated with your software via its powerful API, which makes it the perfect choice for ongoing development.

Installing Vault

The easiest way to install Vault is to download the binary and then configure the path to execute it. To download the correct package, go to www.vaultproject.io/downloads and select the version for your operating system, as shown in Figure 7-1.

Figure 7-1. *The Vault download page*

Download the package and unzip it into a folder. For example, unzip it into a folder called vault and then configure the path to point to your Vault installation.

To check the correct installation of Vault, use the command vault, as shown in Listing 7-1.

Listing 7-1. The Vault Help Commands

```
(base) piggi@piggi:~$ vault
Usage: vault <command> [args]

Common commands:
    read       Read data and retrieves secrets
    write      Write data, configuration, and secrets
    delete     Delete secrets and configuration
    list       List data or secrets
    login      Authenticate locally
    agent      Start a Vault agent
    server     Start a Vault server
    status     Print seal and HA status
```

```
    unwrap        Unwrap a wrapped secret
Other commands:
    audit         Interact with audit devices
    auth          Interact with auth methods
    debug         Runs the debug command
    kv            Interact with Vault's Key-Value storage
    lease         Interact with leases
    namespace     Interact with namespaces
    operator      Perform operator-specific tasks
    path-help     Retrieve API help for paths
    plugin        Interact with Vault plugins and catalog
    policy        Interact with policies
    print         Prints runtime configurations
    secrets       Interact with secrets engines
    ssh           Initiate an SSH session
    token         Interact with tokens
```

The result of the command shows the help list for use with Vault. If the command returns an error like "Command not found," this means the path is not correctly configured and requires correction.

Starting the Vault Dev Server

With Vault installed on your system, the next step is to start the Vault server. Vault is normally operated as client/server software. The Vault server is the only piece of architecture that interacts with the back end and the data storage. All other operations are executed via the CLI or API. All communication uses a TLS standard for secure communication.

The Vault server can start in two ways:

1. *Developer*: This is used primarily for development, testing, or feature exploration. This specific configuration is not very secure. This is because every secret is stored in memory, and Vault is automatically unsealed.

2. *Standard*: This for the normal usage of Vault. With this
   configuration, you need to specify a configuration file. In that file
   it is possible to specify where the secrets are stored, for example,
   and Vault is automatically sealed.

To start a Vault server in Dev mode, it's necessary to use the flag -dev at the
command line:

```
vault server -dev
```

The result of the command is the information for the Vault server start; see Listing 7-2.

Listing 7-2. The Vault Server Running

```
==> Vault server configuration:

             Api Address: http://127.0.0.1:8200
                     Cgo: disabled
         Cluster Address: https://127.0.0.1:8201
              Listener 1: tcp (addr: "127.0.0.1:8200", cluster address:
                          "127.0.0.1:8201", max_request_duration: "1m30s", max_request_
                          size: "33554432", tls: "disabled")
               Log Level: info
                   Mlock: supported: false, enabled: false
           Recovery Mode: false
                 Storage: inmem
                 Version: Vault v1.4.2

WARNING! dev mode is enabled! In this mode, Vault runs entirely in-memory
and starts unsealed with a single unseal key. The root token is already
authenticated to the CLI, so you can immediately begin using Vault.

You may need to set the following environment variable:

PowerShell:
    $env:VAULT_ADDR="http://127.0.0.1:8200"
cmd.exe:
    set VAULT_ADDR=http://127.0.0.1:8200
```

The unseal key and root token is displayed below in case you want to seal/unseal the Vault or re-authenticate.

Unseal Key: MbeCtRzum2LYRbPvMYOtxNwdNywKOkuf4x9flZdQGzo=
Root Token: s.LUiO8tMSOAGcNcfdxoRli8u6

Development mode should NOT be used in production installations!

==> Vault server started! Log data will stream in below:

The result of the startup of the server shows you some important information. The first information you need is the command to export the variable and run the server UI. This command uses these lines:

PowerShell:
    $env:VAULT_ADDR="http://127.0.0.1:8200"
cmd.exe:
    set VAULT_ADDR=http://127.0.0.1:8200

The command line shows the code for a Windows environment. In a Linux environment, the command line to export the value is export VAULT_ADDR='http://127.0.0.1:8200'.

The other important values are the *unseal key* and the *root token*. These values need to be saved because you need to enter them in the UI and unseal the key. To access the UI, you need to open a browser and insert the address http://127.0.0.1:8200, as shown in Figure 7-2.

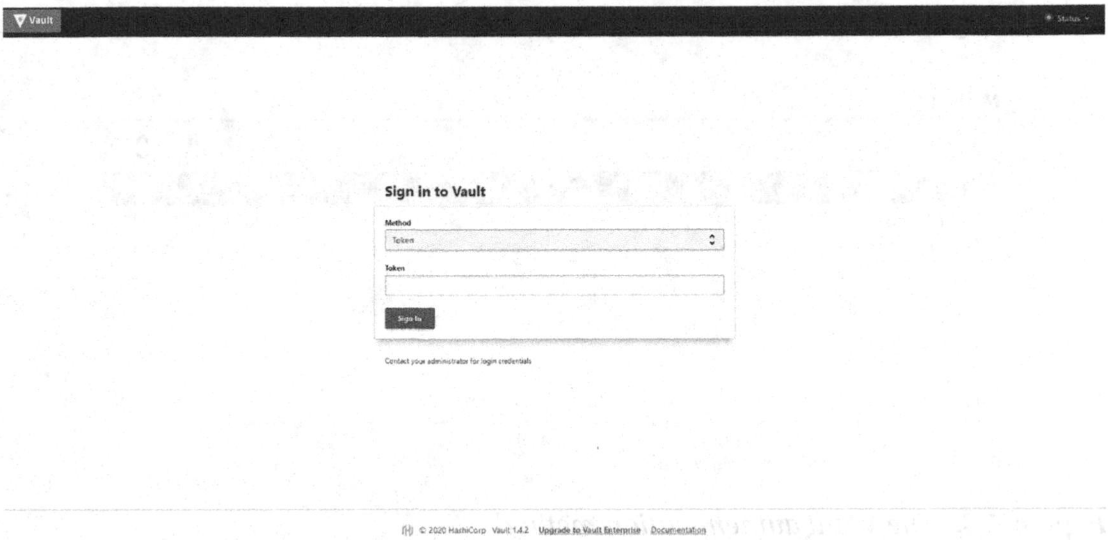

Figure 7-2. *The Vault UI interface*

The UI displays the Vault functionality. The first value of note is the *status* on the right side. In our case, it is green, which means the Vault secrets are *unsealed.* This means Vault has the master key to decrypt the secrets and it is stored in the system.

In our Vault environment, the status is unsealed because we ran a dev Vault environment. If you run a standard Vault configuration, the secret is *sealed* until you *unseal* the system, which is done with the *unseal key.*

To enter the system, you need to sign into Vault. If you click the Method dropbox, it is possible to see the different ways to authenticate on the system; see Figure 7-3.

Sign in to Vault

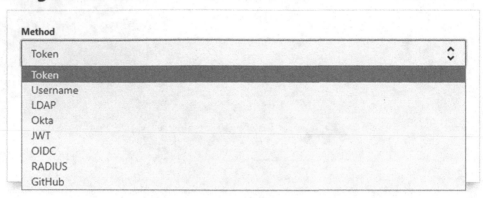

Contact your administrator for login credentials

Figure 7-3. *The Vault authentication method*

In our case, we used the *Token* authentication method. The value for the token is the *root token* you get when you start the server; insert the value and enter, as shown in Figure 7-4.

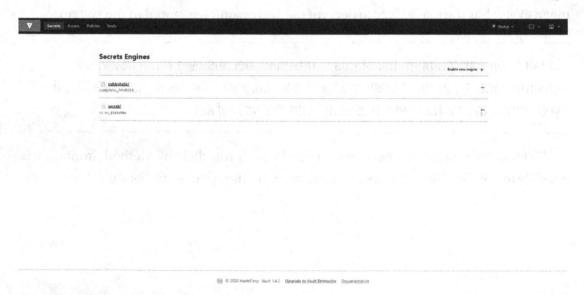

Figure 7-4. *The secrets engines UI*

With the Vault server started, you need to finish the configuration of the server to be used via the CLI. The first step is to configure the address for the Vault server. The steps to export the server are described in the output of the server itself. In a Windows configuration, they are the commands

PowerShell:

```
    $env:VAULT_ADDR="http://127.0.0.1:8200"
```
cmd.exe:

```
    set VAULT_ADDR=http://127.0.0.1:8200
```

To configure, open another command line and execute the command to set the value. Another configuration you need to do is the root token. The command for configuring the root token follows (note that because this command is a command line to configure the operating system, it can be only executed in a command line interface for the operating system):

PowerShell:

```
    $env: VAULT_DEV_ROOT_TOKEN_ID="<your root key>"
```
cmd.exe:

```
    set VAULT_DEV_ROOT_TOKEN_ID="<your root key>"
```
Linux:

```
    export VAULT_DEV_ROOT_TOKEN_ID="<your root key>"
```

The export of the key VAULT_DEV_ROOT_TOKEN_ID allows you to directly log into Vault without using the command vault login. This is fine when you are in a Vault dev server, but must to be avoided when you are in a production environment.

With the export command executed, it is possible to use the command status. To check the status, open a new command line and write the command vault status:

```
Key              Value
---              -----
Seal Type        shamir
Initialized      true
Sealed           false
Total Shares     1
Threshold        1
Version          1.4.2
Cluster Name     vault-cluster-79b74047
Cluster ID       4303fde4-9f5b-3b8e-0ade-61fa604fda95
HA Enabled       false
```

This is the result of the status for the Vault server. With the server reachable and configured via the CLI, it is possible to use the command line to create your first secret.

Managing Your First Secret

With the server up and running, it is time to create your first secret in Vault. It is possible to create a secret in Vault in two ways:

- *Via UI*: You connect on the server via browser and you create a secret.

- *Via CLI*: You connect on the server via the command line and you create a secret.

For the scope of the book, we will use the CLI for the creation of secrets as this allows the use of the HCL language for configuring the application and generating the secrets.

Managing secrets is one of the core features of Vault. The secrets are stored securely, which means all secrets are encrypted first, before they are written into the storage. This means the actual storage you chose is never made clear. The data storage can be a disk, a file, or a Consul cluster.

We are running a dev server, which means the secrets are written in memory. If you use a standard server, it is possible to configure where the secrets are actually stored.

To manage secrets in Vault, you can use the kv object. This object allows the creation, deletion, or retrieval of a secret from the data storage. The first operation to learn is how to write a secret. Use this syntax:

```
vault kv <operation> <path of the secret> <secret>
```

The *operation* is the operation allowed by the kv object. These operations are *put*, *get*, and *delete*. The *path of the secret* is essentially where Vault stores the secret. In Vault, every object is stored in a path that is similar to a virtual file system; think of the path as the folder on your hard disk where you store and organize the secret. The *secret* is what you want to store in a key/value format. Here is an example of a kv object:

```
vault kv put secret/hello first=world
```

The result of the command is shown in Listing 7-3.

Listing 7-3. The Result of the Newly Created Secret

```
Key              Value
---              -----
created_time     2020-05-25T21:48:29.243271639Z (1)
deletion_time    n/a (2)
destroyed        false (3)
version          1 (4)
```

The secret is now created on the system. The result shows some basic information about the secret, such as the creation time (1), the deletion time (2), status (3), and the version (4). The version indicates how many times the secret was recreated. If you execute the same command again, you can see how the version changes:

```
~$ vault kv put secret/hello first=world
Key              Value
---              -----
created_time     2020-05-25T22:02:39.653595677Z
deletion_time    n/a
destroyed        false
version          2
```

When the secret is created, it is possible to create more than one secret at a time:

```
~$ vault kv put secret/hello first=world foo=new
Key              Value
---              -----
created_time     2020-05-25T22:12:02.759354606Z
deletion_time    n/a
destroyed        false
version          3
```

With the secret created, it is possible to check the secret using the get command. To get the secret, use the syntax *vault kv get <path of the secret>*, as in

```
vault kv get secret/hello
```

The result of this command shows all of the secrets under the path. See Listing 7-4.

Listing 7-4. The Result of the Command kv get

```
vault kv get secret/hello
====== Metadata ======
Key                 Value
---                 -----
created_time        2020-05-31T13:24:29.443458143Z
deletion_time       n/a
destroyed           false
version             3

==== Data ====
Key        Value
---        -----
first      world
foo        new
```

The result shows all the information about the secret under the path `secret/hello`, showing the two couple key/values.

The secrets in Vault are stored in data storage. In this scenario, since we are running a dev server, the secrets are stored in memory. When Vault gets a secret, the engine decrypts the secret and shows it to the user. We can see the secret are in a key/value form and because of that, we can see if a secret is presently using the key value of the secret. To get a specific value from a secret, you need to use the option `field`:

```
vault kv get -field=foo secret/hello
```

The result shows the specific value associated with the key:

```
vault kv get -field=foo secret/hello
new
```

With the command kv get, it's possible to parse the output in a JSON format. This functionality is very useful when you want to integrate Vault with another system. To format the output in JSON, you need to use the option `format`. You can now change the previous command to get the output in a JSON format:

```
vault kv get -format=json secret/hello
```

The result is the information about the secret in a JSON format. See Listing 7-5.

Listing 7-5. The Result of the Command hello in a JSON Format

```
{
  "request_id": "4de2a61b-18db-534b-1ab3-d4ff3b751180",
  "lease_id": "",
  "lease_duration": 0,
  "renewable": false,
  "data": {
    "data": {
      "first": "world",
      "foo": "new"
    },
    "metadata": {
      "created_time": "2020-05-31T13:24:29.443458143Z",
      "deletion_time": "",
      "destroyed": false,
      "version": 3
    }
  },
  "warnings": null
}
```

You just learned how to create and read secrets. The last command you need to learn is how to delete a secret. The command to delete a secret is the word delete followed by the name of the secret:

```
vault kv delete secret/hello
```

The result is a message showing the success of the operation, in case the secret exist:

```
Success! Data deleted (if it existed) at: secret/hello
```

The command delete removes the data from the path but doesn't erase the path itself. If you create a new secret in the same path, you will see the version number of the secret increase, as shown in Listing 7-6.

Listing 7-6. The Secret Recreated in the Path secret/hello

```
vault kv put secret/hello foo=world
```

```
Key                Value
---                -----
created_time       2020-05-31T20:25:39.786729558Z
deletion_time      n/a
destroyed          false
version            4
```

It is possible to check and manage the secret via the UI. Simply connect on the address `https://127.0.0.1:8200` and use the access via token and insert the root key vault initially provided when you ran the server.

Vault's Secrets Engine

One of the main functionalities of Vault is to manage secrets. The component responsible for managing secrets is called a *secrets engine*. It stores data, generates a password, or encrypts data. Each secrets engine has a different functionality. Some of them just store data as in a key/value type; others generate dynamic passwords used to connect with another application; and others generate certificates used to connect applications.

In Vault, it is possible to initialize different secrets engines that are isolated from one another. For example, in the previous section, you used the command `vault kv get secret/hello`. This command is used to access on the secrets engine `secret/` and the path `hello`. Try using this command:

```
vault kv put test/hello a=b
```

With the command, you want to use the secrets engine `test/` and the path `hello` but because you don't have this secrets engine and path, Vault will return an error, as shown in Listing 7-7.

Listing 7-7. The Error Returned by Vault When You Try to Access a Non-Existing Secrets Engine

```
Error making API request.

URL: GET http://127.0.0.1:8200/v1/sys/internal/ui/mounts/test/hello
```

```
Code: 403. Errors:
```

```
* preflight capability check returned 403, please ensure client's policies
grant access to path "test/hello/"
```

Vault uses the path to understand which secrets engine needs to be initialized and where it needs to route the traffic. In the path secret/hello, Vault uses the first part, secret/, to identify the secrets engine and then in the secrets engine, routes the traffic to the path hello. By default, Vault uses Version 2 of the key/value secrets engine and because we run in dev, Vault enables the secrets engine secret/.

To better understand how a secrets engine works, the best starting point is to enable a new secrets engine. The syntax to enable a new secrets engine is *vault secrets enable -path=<name> <type>*.

For example, if you want to enable a new secrets engine called hcl_vault, the command is

```
vault secrets enable -path=hcl_vault kv
```

The result is the confirmation of the enabled secrets engine, as shown in Listing 7-8.

Listing 7-8. The Result of a New Secrets Engine

```
vault secrets enable -path=hcl_vault kv
Success! Enabled the kv secrets engine at: hcl_vault/
```

Vault offers different types of secrets engines. This example uses a k/v type. It is possible to use a different type for your secrets engine. This allows users to save different data in the secrets engine itself.

It is possible to get a list of all the secrets present in Vault with the command list:

```
vault secrets list
```

The result is the list of all of the secrets actually present in Vault, as shown in Listing 7-9.

Listing 7-9. The Result of the Vault Secret List

Path	Type	Accessor	Description
cubbyhole/	cubbyhole	cubbyhole_a8267576	per-token private secret storage
hcl_vault/	kv	kv_ae94a7ea	n/a
identity/	identity	identity_fb72a403	identity store
secret/	kv	kv_ac513a90	key/value secret storage
sys/	system	system_697c29b4	system endpoints used for control, policy and debugging

With the new secrets engine enabled, it is possible to create new secrets inside it:

```
vault kv put hcl_vault/hello hello=world
```

The command put returns the status of the command; see Listing 7-10.

Listing 7-10. The Secret Created in the New Secrets Engine

```
vault kv put hcl_vault/hello hello=world
Success! Data written to: hcl_vault/hello
```

It is possible to disable a secrets engine using the command disabled. The command line code for disabling a secret is

```
vault secrets disable hcl_vault/
```

The result is a success message from Vault indicating that the secret is disabled:

```
Success! Disabled the secrets engine (if it existed) at: hcl_vault/
```

When a secrets engine is disabled, all secrets inside are disabled as well. This means it is not possible to access them. In Vault, a secrets engine is similar to a virtual file system. When you execute an operation to read/write/delete/list, Vault uses the first part of the path to identify the secrets engine and then forwards the command to the correct one. When the secrets engine receives the command, it simply executes the operation and returns the result.

Types of Secrets Engines

The type of secrets engine must be specified when it is created. Vault has three families of secrets engines:

1. *General*

2. *Cloud*

3. *Infrastructure*

The *general* type is further divided into five subtypes:

1. *KV*: This is what you've used until now. With this secrets engine you can store key/value secret.

2. *PKI certificate*: This is used to register PKI certificates. This specific secrets engine generates dynamic X.509 certificates. With this secrets engine an application can use Vault to obtain a valid connection, in this case a certificate, without any manual processing.

3. *SSH*: The SSH type secrets engine is used to create an SSH connection between machines. There are two further subtypes: signed SSH-certificate and one-time SSH passwords.

4. *Transit*: This type of secrets engine is used to encrypt data in transit. This service can be viewed like a "Cryptography as Service."

5. *TOTP*: The TOTP type is used to generate a temporary secret following the TOTP standard. This secrets engine can also be used to generate a key and use it validate the password generated by that key. The TOTP can also be used as a password generator similar to Google Authenticator and as a validator like Google's sign-in service.

The *cloud* secrets engines are used to connect the main cloud infrastructure. Under this family of secrets engines it is possible to find

1. *Active Directory*: The AD is a plug-in that can be installed from this path: `https://github.com/hashicorp/vault-plugin-secrets-ad`. This secrets engine has two main functionalities:

- *Password rotation*: The AD secrets engine dynamically rotates the password for AD without any human intervention.

- *Service account check-out*: This feature enables a library of services to be checked out by a human or a service. Vault automatically rotates the password each time the service is checked out.

2. *AliCloud*: The AliCloud secrets engine is designed to connect the Alibaba Cloud. This secret creates an access token based on the RAM (remote access management) policies or AliCloud STS credentials. These tokens are time-based and Vault automatically revokes and regenerates the credentials for us.

3. *AWS*: The AWS secrets engine generates AWS access credentials dynamically based on IAM policies. The AWS IAM credentials are time-based and Vault automatically revokes them when the lease ends.

4. *Google Cloud*: This secrets engine dynamically generates Google Cloud service account keys and OAuth tokens based on IAM policies.

5. *Google Cloud KMS*: This secrets engine provides encryption and key management via Google Cloud KMS (key management service). This engine supports key management, rotation, creation, revocation, encryption, and decryption.

6. Azure: This secrets engine dynamically generates Azure service principals as well as roles and groups. The generated Vault role can be mapped to one or more Azure roles. Each service principals is associated with a Vault lease and when the lease expires, Vault automatically deletes it.

The last family of secrets is the Infrastructure type one. They are used to connect the basic infrastructure type, such as:

1. *Consul*: This type of secrets engine is used to generate Consul API tokens dynamically based on the Consul ACL policies.

2. *Database*: This secrets engine is used to create the credentials to connect databases. The credentials are dynamically created and based on the configuration roles. There are different types of databases that can be connected with Vault. Because Vault supports different types of databases, any database can have a different type of configuration.

3. *Nomad*: This secret is used to generate the Nomad API token based on preexisting ACL policies.

4. *Rabbit MQ*: This type of secrets engine is used to generate user credentials dynamically based on the host configuration. This is possible because with Vault it is possible to configure a virtual host without adding any hard-coded credentials.

These multiple secrets engines make Vault highly versatile and configurable. Most of the secrets engines need to be enabled first to be used. When the secrets engine is enabled, it is possible to use it and then integrate Vault with the application you intend to secure.

Authentication and Authorization in Vault

We have presented the basic utilities of Vault, in particular how to create/manage the secrets and the basic types of secrets engines that are available.

In Vault, we can authenticate using different methods. These different types of authentication are designed to connect Vault with back-end software and allow the developer and architect to integrate Vault with their applications.

Authentication is the process by which the user or machine asks Vault to authenticate itself against an internal or an external system. Vault offers a different authentication method which can be used to solve a specific use case. It is mostly dependent of the type of type of security pattern you want to implement. See Figure 7-5.

Sign in to Vault

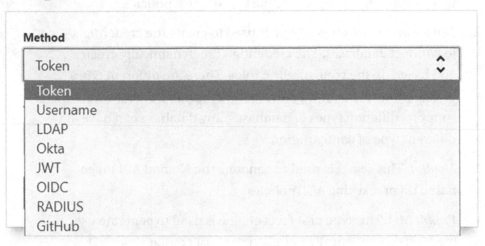

Contact your administrator for login credentials

Figure 7-5. *The different Vault auth methods*

In Vault, before a client can start to interact with Vault itself, it needs to be *authenticated.* The authentication is done against one of the authentication methods Vault offers. Specific authentication methods just need to be enabled in the back end. The authentication is important for understanding *who* is accessing the software. The next important step of the process is *authorization.* Vault uses a different form of authentication, which is done via the different auth method. The *authorization* is the process where Vault determines if the user or the machine is allowed to access a specific path and what operation the user/machine can do in this path.

Vault uses *policies* to define the different authorizations for a specific user or machine logged into Vault. There are some predefined policies that can't be deleted, such as *root* and *default.* The *default* policy is used to associate some basic set of permissions and is associated with all tokens by default. The *root* policy is used to give a token for the superuser admin privileges. This is similar to giving root permission in a Linux machine. The policy is written using HCL but of course JSON is also compatible.

Writing an HCL Policy

The policy is used to define the authorization on the path and to authorize a specific user to define what operations can be executed on a specific path. The secrets are stored on something similar to a virtual path, for example `hello/world`, and for this reason, the policy is crucial for defining the correct access the secrets. The HCL for writing a policy is shown in Listing 7-11.

Listing 7-11. The Basic HCL Used to Write a Policy

```
path "<PATH>" {
  capabilities = [ "<LIST_OF_CAPABILITIES>" ]
}
```

The HCL for a policy defines the Access Common List (ACL) for a specific *path* is where the secret is stored. The *capabilities* define what action can be executed on that specific path. Imagine you want to define a policy for read-only and one with all the access to the path `hcl_vault`; see Listing 7-12.

Listing 7-12. The HCL Policy Used for Read-Only Access

```
path "secret/hcl_vault/*"{
     capabilities =["read"]
}
```

The first policy file defines the "read" access to the path `secret/hcl_vault/*`. The * after `hcl_vault` indicates any secret under the path `hcl_vault`. The policy directly applies to a user or a machine, for example a specific application like Kubernetes or any other application, and this means every user who has this policy can only read the path. The second policy you need to define is for full access on the same path; see Listing 7-13.

Listing 7-13. The HCL Policy for Giving Full Control to the Path

```
,
path "secret/hcl_vault/*"{
     capabilities = ["create", "read", "update", "delete", "list",
     "sudo"]
}
```

When you write a policy, you can use a different syntax to define what path the policy is applied to. This is done using the wildcard character, *. For example, you can define a path for a policy like `secret/hcl_*`. This is used for all paths starting with `hcl_`.

The capabilities are connected to an HTTP verb, and it is used to define the operation allowed via the API call. See Table 7-1.

Table 7-1.   *The Capabilities-Verbs Associations*

Capability	HTTP Verb
Create	POST/PUT
Read	GET
Update	POST/PUT
Delete	DELETE
List	LIST

In addition to the verbs, there are two capabilities not mapped with an HTTP verb. These capabilities are

1. *Sudo*: This is used to access paths that are root-protected. These paths are under `sys/` `pki/` and `auth/`.

2. *Deny*: This is used to disallow access.

In Vault, the policies are additive. This means one capability is added to another until we have the full capability. In case of *deny*, it overrides all the other policies and denies access on the full path.

With HCL, you create your policy in Vault. The syntax to create a policy is

```
vault policy write <POLICY_NAME> <POLICY_FILE>
```

where *POLICY_NAME* is the name associated with the policy and *POLICY_FILE* is the policy file created for defining the policy itself.

Creating Your First Policy

Creating a policy in Vault follows the workflow shown in Figure 7-6.

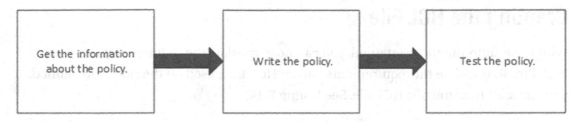

Figure 7-6. *The workflow for creating and implement a policy*

The first step to write a policy is to *get the information about the policy.* In this phase, you define the rules for the policy. For example, you can define your new policy as follows:

- *Administrator*: The administrator role is used to manage all aspects of the Vault infrastructure. The user who has this role can do the following:

  - Enable and manage the auth method on the Vault infrastructure.

  - Enable and manage secrets across the Vault infrastructure.

  - Create and manage ACLs.

  - Perform system health checks.

- *User*: The user is the normal user for the Vault infrastructure. This role can be assigned to an automatic tool for provisioning new servers. The user's privileges consist of these abilities:

  - Mount and manage authorization on the back end.

  - Mount and manage the secrets on the back end.

  - Create and manage the ACL policy.

What we have described is a basic example of how to define the policy for a system. This can be defined for every system because it is generic but in our case, we use this policy for Vault. To correctly define a policy, you need to create a file for any policy, which facilitates easy maintenance of the policy. The next step is to translate the requirements into HCL policy files for Vault.

Creating the HCL File

With the requirements ascertained, you can now translate the requirements into your HCL file. To translate the requirements into an HCL file based on the rules you defined, you can start to define the HCL file. See Listing 7-14.

Listing 7-14. The Administrator HCL Policy

```
path "auth/*" (1)
{
  capabilities = ["create", "read", "update", "delete", "list", "sudo"]
}

path "sys/auth/*" (2)
{
  capabilities = ["create", "update", "delete", "sudo"]
}

path "sys/auth" (3)
{
  capabilities = ["read"]
}

path "sys/policies/acl" (4)
{
  capabilities = ["list"]
}

path "sys/policies/acl/*" (5)
{
  capabilities = ["create", "read", "update", "delete", "list", "sudo"]
}

path "secret/*" (6)
{
  capabilities = ["create", "read", "update", "delete", "list", "sudo"]
}

path "sys/mounts/*" (7)
```

```
{
  capabilities = ["create", "read", "update", "delete", "list", "sudo"]
}

path "sys/mounts" (8)
{
  capabilities = ["read"]
}

path "sys/health" (9)
{
  capabilities = ["read", "sudo"]
}
```

The file `administrator.hcl` implements all of the rules you defined in the administrator policy.

The lines of code from (1) to (3) are used to implement the requirement *"Enable and manage auth method on all of the Vault infrastructure."* Implementation of this policy is done in different steps. The first step is applied on the path `auth/*`. This is the path where all secrets are created. When you define your policy, the requirement for the policy is to enable and maintain all the objects where the policy is applied. Because of this, you need to be sure the auth has the right policy. Line (2) applies the policy to the path `/sys/auth`, which is the path where you create and manage the `auth` method on the back end.

The `/sys/` path is where the back-end objects live in Vault. This means to fully meet the requirement of enabling and managing the `auth/` method, you need to authorize as well `/sys/auth` and `/sys/policy`. The path `/sys/policy/` is responsible for showing the list of polices defined in the system. Lines (4) and (5) authorize the role of *administrator* to read and manage all the ACL(s). This means the administrator can manage and see all of the ACLs defined.

Line (6) enables the CRUD operations on the `secret/` path. This path is the basic home for all of the secrets, and the administrator needs to be able to manage all of the secrets under this path. Lines (7) and (8) are used to manage the secrets engine. The `sys/mounts` path is used to manage the secrets engine. This policy allows the administrator to create and manage the new secrets engines required for the maintenance of the infrastructure.

With the policies created, you can now create the policy in the Vault server. The command used to create the policy is

```
vault policy write POLICY_NAME POLICY_FILE
```

where the POLICY_NAME is the name you want to assign to the policy, for example *admin*, and the POLICY_FILE is the HCL file created to implement the policy such as administrator.hcl:

```
vault policy write admin administrator.hcl
```

The result informs you that the policy has been correctly created:

```
vault policy write admin administrator.hcl
Success! Uploaded policy: admin
```

If you want to see the policies applied to the system, you can use the command list:

```
vault policy list

admin
default
root
```

You can see that the new policy *admin* was created on the system. Finally, to define your new policy, you need to implement the *user* policy, as shown in Listing 7-15.

Listing 7-15. The User Policy, user.hcl

```
path "auth/*"
{
  capabilities = ["create", "read", "update", "delete", "list", "sudo"]
}

path "sys/auth/*"
{
  capabilities = ["create", "update", "delete", "sudo"]
}

path "sys/auth"
```

```
{
  capabilities = ["read"]
}

path "sys/policies/acl"
{
  capabilities = ["list"]
}

path "sys/policies/acl/*"
{
  capabilities = ["create", "read", "update", "delete", "list", "sudo"]
}

path "secret/*"
{
  capabilities = ["create", "read", "update", "delete", "list"]
}
```

You can see that the user policy is similar to the administrator. The difference is what the user can do on the system level. The user does not have any policy on the sys/mount and by default this means it is denied to them.

Conclusion

In this chapter, you explored HashiCorp Vault. This software of the HashiCorp family is used to generate and manage secrets. A secret can be a combination of key/value(s) or other secrets. Vault can be used to generate access to other application(s). In the new multi-cloud architecture, it is essential to have a high level of security, and Vault is crucial. In the next chapter, you will start work on a complete IaC solution including all the HashiCorp products.

CHAPTER 8

Infrastructure as Code with HCL

Infrastructure as Code has become more relevant, which in turn has led to the increased adoption of HashiCorp products. In this chapter, you will learn how to use the HashiCorp product suite to design and implement full Infrastructure as Code.

Infrastructure as Code 101

Chapter 4 provided a short introduction to Infrastructure as Code. It is now time to use HashiCorp software to build IaC.

The main goal for IaC is to have a fully replicable and automated environment. When you decide to adopt IaC, you need to plan and design the infrastructure first to "code" it. A good IaC involves these steps:

1. *Design:* The first step is to formulate the code but a parallel objective is to nail down how the various infrastructure components interact with each other.

2. *Implementation:* To finish the design, you need to implement the infrastructure in parallel, as stated. In this phase, the infrastructure is coded to make it repeatable and testable. Development principles are important during this process.

3. *Release:* Using standard software engineering release principles, the IaC is released.

© Pierluigi Riti and David Flynn 2021
P. Riti and D. Flynn, *Beginning HCL Programming*, https://doi.org/10.1007/978-1-4842-6634-2_8

To release Infrastructure as Code, you must follow the same principles for any software release. The principle you want to follow for your IaC implementation is ***KISS:*** Keep It Simple, Stupid. This principle was first announced by the US Navy in 1960. The KISS principle states that most systems work better if we make them simple, without any unnecessary complexity and overcomplication. Another important principle to keep in mind is the ***DRY*** principle. DRY is an acronym for *Don't Repeat Yourself*, which is a suite of software development principles used to minimize repetition of the software pattern.

As stated, when you create IaC, you are "coding" what you want for your server, such as the database, network configuration, etc. Every IaC system can be defined as follows:

1. *Script:* The script used for the normal maintenance of the system such as changing the network configuration or system configuration.

2. *Configuration management:* IaC relies on configuration management like Ansible or Chef. These tools are the backbone for the automatic release of software.

3. *Templating:* IaC is used to define a template for the server you want to build. This allows quick builds with minimal effort and no duplication. The templating tools are, for example, Packer, Docker, or Vagrant.

4. *Server releasing:* The IaC can be released with Terraform and then deployed on the cloud.

It would appear that IaC requires a large number of tools but this is core to implementing a good DevOps practice in the company. HashiCorp offers a complete set of tools.

IaC offers some improvements on the infrastructure management:

1. *Autonomy*: When you adopt IaC, every team is able to design their own infrastructure. This removes the bottleneck of the classic style of installation where only the SysAdmin team knows how to install the software. With IaC, every team has the capability to install the infrastructure in complete autonomy.

2. *Speed*: The goal of IaC is to have a computer release the infrastructure instead of a human. The system will always execute the same repetitive operation, in a more reliable and efficient way.

3. *Documentation*: IaC follows the same rules used when software is released in that documentation is released at the same juncture.

4. *Versioning*: IaC writes software that defines your infrastructure. These files can be saved in a repository that can be versioned hence versioning your infrastructure.

5. *Security*: The IaC is written in a file used to define all of the capability of the infrastructure. This file can be seen as a piece of code; because of that, you can use specific software to check the file and then isolate and identify the security issues that may be introduced in your infrastructure. For example, it is possible to use the SonarQube plugin to scan the file.

6. *Reuse*: IaC facilitates principles like DRY and KISS. These principles allow you to write code that can be reused for other components of the infrastructure. For example, if you need to release similar infrastructure but to another cloud provider, you can rewrite only that section of code particular for that cloud provider.

IaC offers significant benefits and improvements. The next steps are to define and design what you want to do with your IaC.

Designing the IaC

Implementation of IaC requires design. To achieve this in the cloud, you can use the following tools. These tools are used to create your own IaC:

- *Vagrant*

- *Vault*

- *Consul*

Each tool covers a specific piece of the IaC architecture.

Vagrant is used to create and release a version of the image, called Box, you intend to deploy on the server. The image can be deployed in a different environment and provides the stability of always deploying the same configuration with the same version of the image.

Consul manages the networking tasks and checks the status of the application on the cloud. The last piece of software is *Vault,* which is used for secret management such as passwords for access to different services.

The aim of this chapter is to bring together what you have learned until now to create a full IaC. It is not intended to be production-ready but it is a starting point. The rest of the chapter is mainly focused on the development and design of the IaC. The HashiCorp software covers the server templating and release. The principles used to develop the script are DRY and KISS, emphasizing software design principles.

Defining the Infrastructure

The first step is to define the architecture of your infrastructure. For your project, you need to define the different layers of the architecture and how to integrate it. Let's define the architecture shown in Figure 8-1.

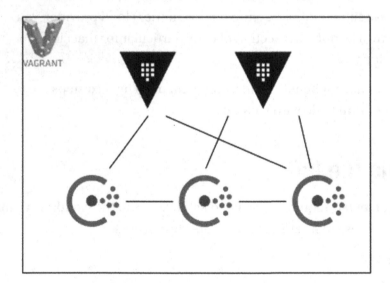

Figure 8-1. *A Vault cluster architecture*

The architecture you are implementing is essentially a Vault high-availability architecture. To implement this architecture, you use Vagrant to create the virtual machines you need for the Consul cluster and the Vault nodes. With Vagrant, you create the Boxes where you install and configure Vault and Consul. This creates the architecture on your local machine. Then you use Terraform to provide the same architecture on the cloud.

The architecture you want to implement is essentially a Vault cluster because you want to implement it on your local machine. You use Vagrant to create the different pieces of architecture.

Vault can be run in a high-availability mode. This mode is designed to protect Vault from an outage. In HA mode, you can replicate the Vault server and then make it available in any condition. In order to run Vault in HA, you need to have a Consul cluster to manage the network behind Vault. To create a Consul cluster, you need at least three Consul nodes, and the only way to have three nodes in a single machine is to use virtual nodes.

Let's create the virtual machines with Vagrant. With Vagrant, you can create and configure Consul and the Vault nodes, and enabled them to communicate with each other.

This type of configuration helps you create a development configuration. This configuration can be utilised to develop what is needed initially to proceed with Terraform to move to the cloud.

Creating the Vagrant File

The first step to create a Vault HA is to create a Consul cluster. This consists of at least three nodes in order have a correct leader election.

The best way to create a Consul cluster in your machine is to use Vagrant to create the different nodes of the cluster. The first step is to create a folder where you create the Vagrant file with the instructions to create the Consul cluster. In the command line, create a folder called hcl_book. For example, in our Ubuntu box, we used this command:

```
mkdir hcl_book
```

Then you need to create the Vagrant file for the cluster. Open your preferred editor and create the Vagrant file with the content in Listing 8-1.

Listing 8-1. The Vagrantfile to Create a Consul Cluster

```
$configuration_script = <<SCRIPT
echo "Installing dependencies for Consul ..."
sudo apt-get update
sudo apt-get install -y unzip curl jq dnsutils
echo "Determining Consul version to install ..."
CHECKPOINT_URL="https://checkpoint-api.hashicorp.com/v1/check"
if [ -z "$CONSUL_DEMO_VERSION" ]; then
CONSUL_DEMO_VERSION=$(curl -s "${CHECKPOINT_URL}"/consul | jq .current_
version | tr -d '"')
fi
echo "Fetching Consul version ${CONSUL_DEMO_VERSION} ..."
cd /tmp/
curl -s https://releases.hashicorp.com/consul/${CONSUL_DEMO_VERSION}/
consul_${CONSUL_DEMO_VERSION}_linux_amd64.zip -o consul.zip
echo "Installing Consul version ${CONSUL_DEMO_VERSION} ..."
unzip consul.zip
sudo chmod +x consul
sudo mv consul /usr/bin/consul
sudo mkdir /etc/consul.d
sudo chmod a+w /etc/consul.d
SCRIPT

CONSUL_DEMO_VERSION = ENV['CONSUL_DEMO_VERSION']

DEMO_BOX_NAME = ENV['DEMO_BOX_NAME'] || "debian/stretch64"

VAGRANTFILE_API_VERSION = "2"

Vagrant.configure(VAGRANTFILE_API_VERSION) do |config|
      config.vm.box = DEMO_BOX_NAME

config.vm.provision "shell",
      inline: $configuration_script,
      env: {'CONSUL_DEMO_VERSION' => CONSUL_DEMO_VERSION}
```

```
    config.vm.define "server1" do |server1|
        server1.vm.hostname = "server1"
        server1.vm.network "private_network", ip: "10.1.142.101"
    end

    config.vm.define "server2" do |server2|
        server2.vm.hostname = "server2"
        server2.vm.network "private_network", ip: "10.1.142.102"
    end

    config.vm.define "server3" do |server3|
        server3.vm.hostname = "server3"
        server3.vm.network "private_network", ip: "10.1.142.103"
    end
end
```

The Vagrantfile is built in two different parts. The first part of the script is a bash program used to configure Consul in the Vagrant images. Listing 8-2 shows the code.

Listing 8-2. The bash Script Used to Configure Consul in the Vagrant Box

```
$configuration_script = <<SCRIPT
echo "Installing dependencies for Consul..."
sudo apt-get update
sudo apt-get install -y unzip curl jq dnsutils
echo "Determining Consul version to install ..."
CHECKPOINT_URL="https://checkpoint-api.hashicorp.com/v1/check"
if [ -z "$CONSUL_DEMO_VERSION" ]; then
CONSUL_DEMO_VERSION=$(curl -s "${CHECKPOINT_URL}"/consul | jq .current_
version | tr -d '"')
fi
echo "Fetching Consul version ${CONSUL_DEMO_VERSION} ..."
cd /tmp/
curl -s https://releases.hashicorp.com/consul/${CONSUL_DEMO_VERSION}/
consul_${CONSUL_DEMO_VERSION}_linux_amd64.zip -o consul.zip
echo "Installing Consul version ${CONSUL_DEMO_VERSION} ..."
unzip consul.zip
sudo chmod +x consul
```

```
sudo mv consul /usr/bin/consul
sudo mkdir /etc/consul.d
sudo chmod a+w /etc/consul.d
SCRIPT
```

The inline shell is the way to write the shell bash command in the Vagrant file. The script allows you to create a script to initiate and configure the machine you want to provide with Vagrant. In this specific case, the script is responsible for downloading and installing Consul in the machine.

The shell script executes some basic steps. Because we used a Debian box, the first command updates the operating system and installs the dependencies necessary to install Consul. This is done via these two lines:

```
sudo apt-get update
sudo apt-get install -y unzip curl jq dnsutils
```

When the system is updated, the next command is to get the actual version of Consul and download it:

```
CHECKPOINT_URL="https://checkpoint-api.hashicorp.com/v1/check"
if [ -z "$CONSUL_DEMO_VERSION" ]; then
CONSUL_DEMO_VERSION=$(curl -s "${CHECKPOINT_URL}"/consul | jq .current_
version | tr -d '"')
fi
echo "Fetching Consul version ${CONSUL_DEMO_VERSION} ..."
cd /tmp/
curl -s https://releases.hashicorp.com/consul/${CONSUL_DEMO_VERSION}/
consul_${CONSUL_DEMO_VERSION}_linux_amd64.zip -o consul.zip
```

The first step of the script is to check the actual version of Consul. This is done by calling the Consul API to the HashiCorp site and getting the last version of the software. The last version at the time of writing this book was 1.8.3. The last command of the script is to download the consul.zip file. This is obtained from the HashiCorp release site in the previous script. Since you dynamically found the version of Consul, you need to use this version.

The last part of the script contains the commands necessary to install and configure Consul:

```
unzip consul.zip
sudo chmod +x consul
sudo mv consul /usr/bin/consul
sudo mkdir /etc/consul.d
sudo chmod a+w /etc/consul.d
```

The commands are quite simple; they unzip Consul and execute the commands to permit Consul to execute via the command line. This command is executed by Vagrant and is part of the configuration of the instance.

After the shell script, there is the section responsible for creating the different instances of the machine:

```
CONSUL_DEMO_VERSION = ENV['CONSUL_DEMO_VERSION']

DEMO_BOX_NAME = ENV['DEMO_BOX_NAME'] || "debian/stretch64"

VAGRANTFILE_API_VERSION = "2"

Vagrant.configure(VAGRANTFILE_API_VERSION) do |config|
    config.vm.box = DEMO_BOX_NAME

    config.vm.provision "shell",
    inline: $configuration_script,
    env: {'CONSUL_DEMO_VERSION' => CONSUL_DEMO_VERSION}

    config.vm.define "server1" do |server1|
        server1.vm.hostname = "server1"
        server1.vm.network "private_network", ip: "10.1.142.101"
    end

    config.vm.define "server2" do |server2|
        server2.vm.hostname = "server2"
        server2.vm.network "private_network", ip: "10.1.142.102"
    end

    config.vm.define "server3" do |server3|
        server3.vm.hostname = "server3"
        server3.vm.network "private_network", ip: "10.1.142.103"
    end
end
```

The Vagrant file is quite simple. The Vagrant configuration file starts downloading the base Debian image you want to use in your environment. The inline script is called by these lines:

```
config.vm.provision "shell",
    inline: $configuration_script,
    env: {'CONSUL_DEMO_VERSION' => CONSUL_DEMO_VERSION}
```

The script executes the command defined to install and configure Consul in your local environment. The last part of the Vagrant file is responsible for defining the hostname and the network interface for the Vagrant box. This can be used to allow Consul to communicate with it.

The actual Vagrantfile creates the Consul box. It can be used by Vagrant to create the Consul server of your architecture but it doesn't create the cluster yet. This is the starting point for creating your cluster. To create the full script, it is better to check if the different Consul boxes can talk to each other.

With the Vagrant file ready, you can start the Vagrant box. To run the Vagrant box, use the command `vagrant up`. The result shows the box running:

```
server1: Setting up bind9-host (1:9.10.3.dfsg.P4-12.3+deb9u6) ...
server3: Setting up bind9-host (1:9.10.3.dfsg.P4-12.3+deb9u6) ...
server2: Setting up dnsutils (1:9.10.3.dfsg.P4-12.3+deb9u6) ...
server1: Setting up dnsutils (1:9.10.3.dfsg.P4-12.3+deb9u6) ...
server3: Setting up dnsutils (1:9.10.3.dfsg.P4-12.3+deb9u6) ...
server2: Processing triggers for libc-bin (2.24-11+deb9u4) ...
server1: Processing triggers for libc-bin (2.24-11+deb9u4) ...
server3: Processing triggers for libc-bin (2.24-11+deb9u4) ...
server2: Determining Consul version to install ...
server1: Determining Consul version to install ...
server3: Determining Consul version to install ...
server2: Fetching Consul version 1.8.3 ...
server1: Fetching Consul version 1.8.3 ...
server3: Fetching Consul version 1.8.3 ...
server3: Installing Consul version 1.8.3 ...
server3: Archive:  consul.zip
server3:    inflating: consul
server2: Installing Consul version 1.8.3 ...
```

```
server2: Archive:  consul.zip
server2:    inflating: consul
server1: Installing Consul version 1.8.3 ...
server1: Archive:  consul.zip
server1:    inflating: consul
```

It can be observed that the script executes some operations with the output shown. Now you can create and connect to the Consul cluster.

Connecting to the Consul Box

With Vagrant box operational, you can now connect Consul to create a data center. To connect the different Consul nodes, you need to connect to the box. To connect on the box, use the command ssh:

```
vagrant ssh server1
```

This command opens a connection with the first box and allows you to interact with the underlying operation system. See Listing 8-3.

Listing 8-3. The Result of the Vagrant ssh on server1

```
Linux server1 4.9.0-12-amd64 #1 SMP Debian 4.9.210-1 (2020-01-20) x86_64

The programs included with the Debian GNU/Linux system are free software;
the exact distribution terms for each program are described in the
individual files in /usr/share/doc/*/copyright.

Debian GNU/Linux comes with ABSOLUTELY NO WARRANTY, to the extent
permitted by applicable law.
vagrant@server1:~$
```

The command you use to create the Consul box does not start the agent. The command for starting the agent is this:

```
# vagrant@server1:~
$ consul agent \
  -server \
  -bootstrap-expect=1 \
  -node=agent-one \
```

```
-bind=10.1.142.101 \
-data-dir=/tmp/consul \
-config-dir=/etc/consul.d
```

This starts the Consul agent. The agent is started and you can see the logs for the agent running in Listing 8-4.

Listing 8-4. The Results of Starting the Consul Server

```
BootstrapExpect is set to 1; this is the same as Bootstrap mode.
bootstrap = true: do not enable unless necessary
==> Starting Consul agent...
           Version: '1.8.3'
           Node ID: '369594d4-c96a-11c0-84b5-39f4e100996f'
         Node name: 'agent-one'
        Datacenter: 'dc1' (Segment: '<all>')
            Server: true (Bootstrap: true)
       Client Addr: [127.0.0.1] (HTTP: 8500, HTTPS: -1, gRPC: -1, DNS: 8600)
      Cluster Addr: 10.1.142.101 (LAN: 8301, WAN: 8302)
           Encrypt: Gossip: false, TLS-Outgoing: false, TLS-Incoming:
           false, Auto-Encrypt-TLS: false

==> Log data will now stream in as it occurs:
   2020-09-06T16:54:42.760Z [WARN]  agent.auto_config: BootstrapExpect is
   set to 1; this is the same as Bootstrap mode.
   2020-09-06T16:54:42.760Z [WARN]  agent.auto_config: bootstrap = true:
   do not enable unless necessary
   2020-09-06T16:54:43.087Z [INFO]  agent.server.raft: initial
   configuration: index=1 servers="[{Suffrage:Voter ID:369594d4-c96a-11c0-
   84b5-39f4e100996f Address:10.1.142.101:8300}]"
   2020-09-06T16:54:43.089Z [INFO]  agent.server.serf.wan: serf:
   EventMemberJoin: agent-one.dc1 10.1.142.101
   2020-09-06T16:54:43.090Z [INFO]  agent.server.serf.lan: serf:
   EventMemberJoin: agent-one 10.1.142.101
   2020-09-06T16:54:43.091Z [INFO]  agent: Started DNS server:
   address=127.0.0.1:8600 network=udp
```

```
2020-09-06T16:54:43.091Z [INFO]  agent.server.raft: entering follower
state: follower="Node at 10.1.142.101:8300 [Follower]" leader=
2020-09-06T16:54:43.092Z [INFO]  agent.server: Adding LAN server:
server="agent-one (Addr: tcp/10.1.142.101:8300) (DC: dc1)"
2020-09-06T16:54:43.092Z [INFO]  agent.server: Handled event for server
in area: event=member-join server=agent-one.dc1 area=wan
2020-09-06T16:54:43.093Z [INFO]  agent: Started DNS server:
address=127.0.0.1:8600 network=tcp
2020-09-06T16:54:43.094Z [INFO]  agent: Started HTTP server:
address=127.0.0.1:8500 network=tcp
2020-09-06T16:54:43.094Z [INFO]  agent: started state syncer
```
==> Consul agent running!
```
2020-09-06T16:54:50.381Z [ERROR] agent.anti_entropy: failed to sync
remote state: error="No cluster leader"
2020-09-06T16:54:51.703Z [WARN]  agent.server.raft: heartbeat timeout
reached, starting election: last-leader=
2020-09-06T16:54:51.703Z [INFO]  agent.server.raft: entering candidate
state: node="Node at 10.1.142.101:8300 [Candidate]" term=2
2020-09-06T16:54:51.810Z [INFO]  agent.server.raft: election won:
tally=1
2020-09-06T16:54:51.811Z [INFO]  agent.server.raft: entering leader
state: leader="Node at 10.1.142.101:8300 [Leader]"
2020-09-06T16:54:51.812Z [INFO]  agent.server: cluster leadership
acquired
2020-09-06T16:54:51.812Z [INFO]  agent.server: New leader elected:
payload=agent-one
2020-09-06T16:54:51.911Z [INFO]  agent.leader: started routine:
routine="federation state anti-entropy"
2020-09-06T16:54:51.912Z [INFO]  agent.leader: started routine:
routine="federation state pruning"
2020-09-06T16:54:51.912Z [INFO]  agent.leader: started routine:
routine="CA root pruning"
2020-09-06T16:54:51.912Z [INFO]  agent.server: member joined, marking
health alive: member=agent-one
```

```
2020-09-06T16:54:51.945Z [INFO]  agent.server: federation state anti-
entropy synced
2020-09-06T16:54:53.861Z [INFO]  agent: Synced node info
```

The command line to start the server has some options for defining the cluster. The first option is -server, which starts the node as a server. This is important when the leader needs to be elected. In your case, you want only one server and this is specified by another parameter: -bootstrap-expect=1. This indicates how many servers you expect to have. The other parameter is the name of the agent and the IP address the node responds to; you specify what data dir plus what configuration file you use. With the agent started, another command line is opened with another SSH console with the Vagrant box. Once again, use the command m. With the console opened on server1, you can check how many members you have in your cluster at this juncture:

```
vagrant@server1:~$ consul members
Node        Address             Status  Type    Build  Protocol  DC   Segment
agent-one   10.1.142.101:8301   alive   server  1.8.3  2         dc1  <all>
```

The result in your case is just the first node. To have a cluster, you need to add the other nodes. You need to spin up the other two Consul nodes and join them to the cluster. To join new nodes, you execute commands similar to the ones you used to start the server. The only difference is what parameters you send to spin up the node.

Open another command line and SSH this your second Vagrant box: vagrant ssh server2. You now need to run the command to start the new agent. The configuration for the new agent is shown in Listing 8-5.

Listing 8-5. The Consul Code to Run the New Agent

```
consul agent \
  -node=agent-two \
  -bind=10.1.142.102 \
  -enable-script-checks=true \
  -data-dir=/tmp/consul \
  -config-dir=/etc/consul.d
```

This command is different from what you ran on the server node. In this case, there are fewer options. There is no server or bootstrap option, just a node. When the node is started this time, you'll get some exceptions. This is because the node started as an agent and you didn't join it to any server. See Listing 8-6.

Listing 8-6. The Consul Run for Server2

```
==> Consul agent running!
    2020-09-06T17:09:02.223Z [WARN]  agent.client.manager: No servers
    available
    2020-09-06T17:09:02.223Z [ERROR] agent.anti_entropy: failed to sync
    remote state: error="No known Consul servers"
    2020-09-06T17:09:29.100Z [WARN]  agent.client.manager: No servers
    available
    2020-09-06T17:09:29.100Z [ERROR] agent.anti_entropy: failed to sync
    remote state: error="No known Consul servers"
    2020-09-06T17:09:47.054Z [WARN]  agent.client.manager: No servers
    available
    2020-09-06T17:09:47.055Z [ERROR] agent.anti_entropy: failed to sync
    remote state: error="No known Consul servers"
    2020-09-06T17:10:08.684Z [WARN]  agent.client.manager: No servers
    available
    2020-09-06T17:10:08.685Z [ERROR] agent.anti_entropy: failed to sync
    remote state: error="No known Consul servers"
    2020-09-06T17:10:24.980Z [WARN]  agent.client.manager: No servers
    available
    2020-09-06T17:10:24.980Z [ERROR] agent.anti_entropy: failed to sync
    remote state: error="No known Consul servers"
```

The node is up and running but shows an error. This is because it needs to be joined to a server. The command for joining the node on the server is

```
consul join 10.1.142.101
```

The command `join` accepts the IP address of the server you want to join. The response is just a line to tell you if the node correctly joined the server:

```
vagrant@server2:~$ consul join 10.1.142.101
Successfully joined cluster by contacting 1 nodes.
```

Because you joined the node, you can see the result on the server log of server2:

```
2020-09-06T17:10:49.638Z [INFO]  agent: (LAN) joining: lan_addresses=
[10.1.142.101]
```

171

```
2020-09-06T17:10:49.642Z [INFO]  agent.client.serf.lan: serf:
EventMemberJoin: agent-one 10.1.142.101
2020-09-06T17:10:49.644Z [INFO]  agent: (LAN) joined: number_of_nodes=1
2020-09-06T17:10:49.645Z [INFO]  agent.client: adding server:
server="agent-one (Addr: tcp/10.1.142.101:8300) (DC: dc1)"
2020-09-06T17:10:51.869Z [INFO]  agent: Synced node info
```

With the node joined, you can now return to the command line for the server node and again run the command members. This shows a different result from the first run because you have joined another node. In the server command line, run this command: consul member. The result shows the nodes of the cluster; see Listing 8-7.

Listing 8-7. The Consul Cluster with the Server and One Node

```
vagrant@server1:~$ consul members
Node        Address            Status  Type    Build  Protocol  DC    Segment
agent-one   10.1.142.101:8301  alive   server  1.8.3  2         dc1   <all>
agent-two   10.1.142.102:8301  alive   client  1.8.3  2
dc1   <default>
```

To finish the creation of your cluster, you need to join a third node. Open another command line and run the third instance. When you connect on the Vagrant Consul box, execute the same command you ran for node two. The difference will be the IP address and the name of the node:

```
consul agent \
  -node=agent-three \
  -bind=10.1.142.103 \
  -enable-script-checks=true \
  -data-dir=/tmp/consul \
  -config-dir=/etc/consul.d
```

With this node now running, you need to join it to the cluster. Open another console in agent3 and use the command join to join the node with the server. With the node joined, finally you can use the command members to check all of the nodes on the cluster. See Listing 8-8.

Listing 8-8. The Consul members Command Showing All of the Nodes in the Cluster

```
vagrant@server1:~$ consul members
Node          Address             Status Type    Build Protocol DC    Segment
agent-one     10.1.142.101:8301   alive  server  1.8.3 2        dc1   <all>
agent-three   10.1.142.103:8301   alive  client  1.8.3 2        dc1   <default>
agent-two     10.1.142.102:8301   alive  client  1.8.3 2        dc1   <default>
```

Improving the Consul Cluster

You just designed a basic cluster Consul configuration. This is the first step to create a Vault cluster. But to have a fully automated and near a production-ready cluster, you can't join the cluster automatically and you need more than one simple server. The idea is to modify the script to run Consul. This script is generic and creates a cluster with three servers. See Listing 8-9.

Listing 8-9. The Generic Consul Server Configuration

```
{
  "server": true,
  "node_name": "$NODE_NAME",
  "datacenter": "hcldc",
  "data_dir": "$CONSUL_DATA_PATH",
  "bind_addr": "0.0.0.0",
  "client_addr": "0.0.0.0",
  "advertise_addr": "$ADVERTISE_ADDR",
  "bootstrap_expect": 3,
  "retry_join": ["$SERVER1", "$SERVER2", "$SERVER3"],
  "ui": true,
  "log_level": "DEBUG",
  "enable_syslog": true,
  "acl_enforce_version_8": false
}
```

This is a generic template that can be used to generate your HCL file. The scope is to create three different HCL files that can be used to provide for your cluster. For example, the configuration.hcl is shown in Listing 8-10.

Listing 8-10. The configuration.hcl File

```
server = true
node_name = "server1"
datacentre = "hcldc"
data_dir = "/tmp/consul"
bind_addr = "0.0.0.0"
client_addr = "0.0.0.0"
advertise_addr = "10.1.142.101",
bootstrap_expect = 3
retry_join = ["10.1.142.101", "10.1.142.102", "10.1.142.103"]
ui = true
log_level = "DEBUG"
enable_syslog = true
acl_enforce_version_8 = false
```

You can easily create the other two HCL configurations. Just change the values node_
name, advertise_addr, and the HCL file for server2 to

```
server = true
node_name = "server2"
datacentre = "hcldc"
data_dir = "/tmp/consul"
bind_addr = "0.0.0.0"
client_addr = "0.0.0.0"
advertise_addr = "10.1.142.102",
bootstrap_expect = 3
retry_join = ["10.1.142.101", "10.1.142.102", "10.1.142.103"]
ui = true
log_level = "DEBUG"
enable_syslog = true
acl_enforce_version_8 = false
```

The configuration file for server3 is

```
server = true
node_name = "server3"
datacentre = "hcldc"
data_dir = "/tmp/consul"
```

```
bind_addr = "0.0.0.0"
client_addr = "0.0.0.0"
advertise_addr = "10.1.142.102",
bootstrap_expect = 3
retry_join = ["10.1.142.101", "10.1.142.102", "10.1.142.103"]
ui = true
log_level = "DEBUG"
enable_syslog = true
acl_enforce_version_8 = false
```

With the configuration files now created, you need to change how you create your Consul agent and server. In order to have a correct Vault cluster, you need to have at least three server nodes running and two agents. These two agents are installed where Vault is run.

Creating the Vault Cluster

You have created a basic Consul cluster, but this is just a starting point. To create a Vault cluster, you need to have the Consul cluster and you need to add two Consul clients. The client is used to connect the Vault cluster and give you the high availability for the server.

The new machine we go to configure have in the same machine the Consul client and the Vault node we want to add in the cluster. To make this simple, you have two Vault servers connected with the Consul client/server. To create a new Consul client, use the script in Listing 8-11.

Listing 8-11. The Client Configuration File

```
server = false
datacenter = "hcldc"
node_name = "client1"
data_dir = "/tmp/consul"
bind_addr = "10.1.142.201"
client_addr ="127.0.0.1"
retry_join = ["10.1.142.101", "10.1.142.102", "10.1.142.103"]
log_level = "DEBUG"
enable_syslog =true
acl_enforce_version_8 = false
```

This file is used to create the first client. The second is the same; just change the name and the binding address because is a client, so choose the addresses 201 and 202. Another important difference between the client and the server is the value

```
server = "false"
```

This parameter tells to Consul to run a client and not a server. You now need to create the new HCL file to configure the other client.

With Consul now defined, you need to download and install Vault and configure it to work in the cluster. To install Vault in the same VM where you created the Consul client, you need to execute the script shown in Listing 8-12.

Listing 8-12. The Bash Script Used to Download and Install Vault

```
VAULT_VERSION="$(curl -s https://releases.hashicorp.com/vault/index.json |
jq -r '.versions[].version' | grep -v 'beta\|rc' | tail -n 1)"
VAULT_ZIP="vault_${VAULT_VERSION}_linux_amd64.zip"
VAULT_URL=${URL:-"https://releases.hashicorp.com/vault/${VAULT_
VERSION}/${VAULT_ZIP}"}

curl --silent --output /tmp/${VAULT_ZIP} ${VAULT_URL}

sudo unzip -o /tmp/${VAULT_ZIP} -d /usr/local/bin/
sudo chmod 0755 /usr/local/bin/vault
sudo chown vault:vault /usr/local/bin/vault
sudo mkdir -pm 0755 /etc/vault.d
sudo mkdir -pm 0755 /etc/ssl/vault

sudo chown -R vault:vault /etc/vault.d /etc/ssl/vault
sudo chmod -R 0644 /etc/vault.d/*
echo "export VAULT_ADDR=http://127.0.0.1:8200" | sudo tee /etc/profile.d/
vault.sh
```

This code is put in a separate SH file called `install_vault.sh`. This script is called by the Vagrant file and installs Vault on the client. You now have all the pieces you need, so let's update the Vagrantfile with the script and the new configuration. See Listing 8-13.

Listing 8-13. The New Vagrantfile

```
CONSUL_DEMO_VERSION = ENV['CONSUL_DEMO_VERSION']

DEMO_BOX_NAME = ENV['DEMO_BOX_NAME'] || "debian/stretch64"

VAGRANTFILE_API_VERSION = "2"

Vagrant.configure(VAGRANTFILE_API_VERSION) do |config|
    config.vm.box = DEMO_BOX_NAME

config.vm.provision "shell",
    inline: $configuration_script,
env: {'CONSUL_DEMO_VERSION' => CONSUL_DEMO_VERSION}

    config.vm.define "server1" do |server1|
        server1.vm.hostname = "server1"
        server1.vm.network "private_network", ip: "10.1.142.101"
    end

    config.vm.define "server2" do |server2|
        server2.vm.hostname = "server2"
        server2.vm.network "private_network", ip: "10.1.142.102"
    end

    config.vm.define "server3" do |server3|
        server3.vm.hostname = "server3"
        server3.vm.network "private_network", ip: "10.1.142.103"
    end

  config.vm.define "client1" do |client1|
        client1.vm.hostname = "server1"
        client1.vm.network "private_network", ip: "10.1.142.201"
      client1.vm.network :forwarded_port, guest: 8200, host: 8202, auto_
      correct: true
    end

  config.vm.define "client2" do |client2|
        client2.vm.hostname = "client2"
        client2.vm.network "private_network", ip: "10.1.142.202"
```

```
        client2.vm.network :forwarded_port, guest: 8200, host: 8202, auto_
        correct: true
    end

  config.vm.provision "shell", path: "scripts/install-vault.sh"
end
```

With the new Vagrantfile, you now can execute the full script necessary to install and configure the cluster. The $configuration_script is essentially the script you defined in the previous paragraph. The configuration script is one:

```
VAULT_VERSION="$(curl -s https://releases.hashicorp.com/vault/index.json |
jq -r '.versions[].version' | grep -v 'beta\|rc' | tail -n 1)"
VAULT_ZIP="vault_${VAULT_VERSION}_linux_amd64.zip"
VAULT_URL=${URL:-"https://releases.hashicorp.com/vault/${VAULT_
VERSION}/${VAULT_ZIP}"}

curl --silent --output /tmp/${VAULT_ZIP} ${VAULT_URL}

sudo unzip -o /tmp/${VAULT_ZIP} -d /usr/local/bin/
sudo chmod 0755 /usr/local/bin/vault
sudo chown vault:vault /usr/local/bin/vault
sudo mkdir -pm 0755 /etc/vault.d
sudo mkdir -pm 0755 /etc/ssl/vault

sudo chown -R vault:vault /etc/vault.d /etc/ssl/vault
sudo chmod -R 0644 /etc/vault.d/*
echo "export VAULT_ADDR=http://127.0.0.1:8200" | sudo tee /etc/profile.d/
vault.sh
```

Conclusion

In this chapter, you learned how to use Vagrant to create a complete IaC. This code is far from production-ready, but it gives you a taste of what you can do with the HashiCorp suite if you want to implement a full IaC.

Index

© Pierluigi Riti and David Flynn 2021
P. Riti and D. Flynn, *Beginning HCL Programming*, https://doi.org/10.1007/978-1-4842-6634-2

Printed in the United States
by Baker & Taylor Publisher Services

Printed in the United States
by Baker & Taylor Publisher Services